...blished
...brands,
...Thomas Cook are the experts in travel.

For more than 135 years our guidebooks have unlocked the secrets of destinations around the world, sharing with travellers a wealth of experience and a passion for travel.

Rely on Thomas Cook as your travelling companion on your next trip and benefit from our unique heritage.

Thomas Cook **pocket** guides

VIENNA

Written and updated by Kerry Christiani

Published by Thomas Cook Publishing
A division of Thomas Cook Tour Operations Limited
Company registration no. 3772199 England
The Thomas Cook Business Park, Unit 9, Coningsby Road,
Peterborough PE3 8SB, United Kingdom
Email: books@thomascook.com, Tel: +44 (0) 1733 416477
www.thomascookpublishing.com

Produced by Cambridge Publishing Management Limited
Burr Elm Court, Main Street, Caldecote CB23 7NU
www.cambridgepm.co.uk

Series design based on an original concept by Studio 183 Limited

ISBN: 978-1-84848-375-0

Series Editor: Karen Beaulah
Production/DTP: Steven Collins

Printed and bound in Spain by GraphyCems

CONTENTS

SYMBOLS KEY

The following symbols are used throughout this book:

ⓐ address ⓣ telephone ⓦ website address
opening times public transport connections ❶ important

The following symbols are used on the maps:

i	information office	■	point of interest
	airport	O	city
+	hospital	O	large town
	police station	○	small town
	bus station		motorway
	railway station		main road
U	U-Bahn		minor road
†	cathedral	—	railway
❶	numbers denote featured cafés & restaurants		

Hotels and restaurants are graded by approximate price as follows:
£ budget price **££** mid-range price **£££** expensive

In addresses, 'Strasse' and '-strasse' (meaning 'street' or 'road') are abbreviated to 'Str.' and '-str.'

The Rathaus (Vienna City Hall)

INTRODUCING
Vienna

Introduction

Nostalgic and innovative, romantic and oh-so cultured, Vienna is a city like no other. Nowhere but in the Austrian capital would you find Habsburg palaces sidling up to avant-garde shopping centres and opulent cafés sitting next to über-cool lounge bars. Here, on the banks of the blue Danube immortalised in Strauss's famous waltz, past and present walk hand in hand.

Built high and mighty on the wealth of an empire, Vienna has enthralled visitors for centuries. Today trams still rumble around the tree-fringed Ringstrasse boulevard, horse-drawn traps pull up in front of Gothic giant St Stephen's Cathedral and the Prater's Ferris wheel turns by day and twinkles by night. It won't be long before you start to share the city's obsession with coffee and chocolate cake and its passion for culture.

While classic highlights like the Imperial Palace and Belvedere Gallery still top most must-see lists, a growing crop of imaginative boutiques, offbeat galleries, new-wave restaurants and design hotels is giving the centre a 21st-century kick. But the real beauty of Vienna is the laid-back attitude of the Viennese. Masters in the art of *Gemütlichkeit* (cosiness), Vienna's 1.6 million residents love nothing better than to while away an afternoon in a café, catch up with friends in an inviting *Heurige* (wine tavern) or take a stroll in the city's parks. And you are usually most welcome to join them.

After you've explored the heart of the city, Vienna's green backyard beckons. Edging west, the lush Wienerwald is packed with things to see and do from medieval castles set on limestone crags to sublime Benedictine abbeys and spas. You can spend days discovering the riches of the World Heritage Wachau Valley, just an hour from the city, where steep vines tumble down to the Danube. Dramatic cityscapes and nature trails, all-night parties and pin-drop peace: the Austrian capital has got the lot!

Get fantastic views from the Riesenrad Ferris wheel in Prater Park

When to go

Each season has its own appeal in Vienna. Spring sees the parks in full bloom, while autumn invites long strolls in the woodlands that fringe the city. In summer, Vienna is one big party with open-air film screenings, concerts and festivals. Winter, too, can be magical when the Christmas markets bring a festive sparkle to the city.

SEASONS & CLIMATE

Vienna does not see climatic extremes. Summer temperatures peak at around 25°C (77°F), which is most people's idea of pleasantly warm. In winter, make sure you wrap up since the occasional sub-zero temperatures, which have been known to plummet to –10°C (14°F), can often bring a generous sprinkling of snow. With

Vienna's stunning Staatsoper by night

temperatures hovering between 10° and 15°C (50° and 59°F), spring and autumn are quite mild.

ANNUAL EVENTS

January

New Year's Day Concert in Vienna Catch this world-famous New Year's concert with the Philharmonic Orchestra at Vienna Musikverein's Golden Hall. ⓐ Boesendorfer Str. 12 ⓣ 01 505 65 25 ⓦ www.wienerphilharmoniker.at

Practitioners' Ball Dress up to the nines to attend this sublime ball at the Hofburg Palace. ⓐ Kaisertor/Innerer Burghof ⓣ 01 515 01 12 34 ⓦ www.aerzteball.at

Vienna Ice Dream Get your skates on as the Rathausplatz in front of Vienna's City Hall becomes a giant ice rink. ⓐ Rathausplatz ⓣ 01 40 900 40 ⓦ www.wienereistraum.com

March

Vienna Opera Ball Sounds of Strauss, couples twirling across the floor and plenty of glamour and glitz at the Staatsoper. ⓐ Opernring 2 ⓣ 01 514 44 26 13 ⓦ www.wiener-staatsoper.at

Schönbrunn Easter Fair Stalls selling eggs, toys and wreaths, plus Easter egg hunts and other activities. ⓐ Schönbrunner Schloss Str. ⓣ 01 811 13 239 ⓦ www.schoenbrunn.at

May

City Festival Vienna leaps into spring with this three-day festival. From concerts and clowns to improvised theatre and parties, everything at this fun-fuelled event is free! ⓣ 01 515 430 ⓦ www.stadtfest-wien.at

Sand in the City Head to this urban beach and join the cocktail sippers by the pool. There are regular DJs and salsa parties (runs until Sept). ⓐ Lothringerstrasse ⓦ www.sandinthecity.at

May & June

Vienna Festival Culture vultures flock to this mammoth festival which features a string of theatre and music highlights. ⓣ 01 589 22 22 ⓦ www.festwochen.at

June

Danube Island Festival Three-day festival of free open-air concerts and performances by local and international bands. ⓐ Danube ⓣ 01 535 35 35 ⓦ www.donauinselfest.at

June & July

Jazz Fest Wien (Vienna Jazz Festival) Expect smooth jazz and big talent appearing at venues across Vienna. ⓣ 01 712 42 24 ⓦ www.viennajazz.org

July & August

Vienna International Dance Festival A five-week festival of dance: over 40 performances and more than 200 workshops with companies and choreographers from around the world. Performances throughout Vienna. ⓣ 01 523 55 580 ⓦ www.impulstanz.com

Open-Air Cinema Vienna celebrates summer with free film screenings on squares including Rathausplatz and Karlsplatz (runs until mid-Sept). ⓐ Various city venues ⓦ www.wien.gv.at

October

Viennale Austria's biggest film festival keeps Vienna glued to big screens across the city. ⓐ Siebensterngasse 2 ⓣ 01 526 59 47 ⓦ www.viennale.at

November & December

Christmas Market Nibble on gingerbread and sip mulled wine beneath twinkling trees on Rathausplatz at this 700-year-old festive market. ⓐ Rathausplatz ⓣ 01 245 55 ⓦ www.christkindlmarkt.at

December

Imperial Ball Ringing in the New Year and Vienna's ball season, this is a grand occasion at the Hofburg. ⓐ Kaisertor/Innerer Burghof ⓣ 01 587 36 66 23 ⓦ www.hofburg.com

PUBLIC HOLIDAYS

New Year's Day 1 Jan
Epiphany 6 Jan
Easter Monday 25 Apr 2011; 9 Apr 2012; 1 Apr 2013
National Holiday 1 May
Ascension Day 2 June 2011; 17 May 2012; 9 May 2013
Whit Monday 13 June 2011; 28 May 2012; 20 May 2013
Corpus Christi 23 June 2011; 7 June 2012; 30 May 2013
Assumption 15 Aug
National Holiday 26 Oct
All Saints' Day 1 Nov
Conception 8 Dec
Christmas & Boxing Day 25 & 26 Dec

Vienna Ball season

Whirling through more than 200 balls during the *Fasching* (carnival) period from New Year to late February, Vienna certainly knows how to beat the winter blues with a little sparkle and Strauss. In the birthplace of the waltz, the ball season is firmly rooted in Austrian culture. The glittering decorations, fancy footwork and free-flowing champagne will (quite literally) sweep you off your feet.

The balls range from intimate dos to incredibly grand affairs held at the stately Hofburg Palace (see page 58). Dressing up is usually a must – ties and tails for men and ankle-length dresses for women. If you want to join the fun, but don't have a tux or taffeta ball gown handy, there are a number of places in town that rent out formal wear. Those with two left feet can take expert tips to polish their foxtrot, polka and waltz with dance lessons before the event.

Dazzling in their confidence and finery, Vienna's high society and any other mortals lucky enough to have tickets turn out for the biggies. These include the Imperial Ball, which rings in New Year at the Hofburg Palace and gives participants hopes of a divinely decadent 12 months, the elegant Practitioners' Ball, the Philharmonic Ball, the Kaffeesiederball staged by the capital's coffee houses and, perhaps most famous of all, the sublime Opera Ball, where pink carnations rain down when the orchestra plays *The Blue Danube*. Quirky additions feature the bizarre Wallflower Ball (dress code: drab) and the (anti-) Ball of Bad Taste where the more awful the clothes and dreadful the music the better.

Whether you want to mingle with the glitterati, follow the rhythm of the *polonaise* (the jaunty call to terpsichorean dandyism) or slip into one of the wackier events, you'll need to make sure you book your tickets well in advance (the tourist office provides details, see page 134). Keep an ear resolutely cocked for the opening strains of the rabble-rousing *Alles Waltzer*, your cue to dance.

Couples glide across the floor at the Practitioners' Ball

History

Baroque palaces, formal gardens, stately homes and world-class museums shape what was once the epicentre of the Habsburg Empire. While the capital is best known for its imperial clout, its road to success hasn't always been smooth. On the crossroads of trade routes between East and West, it was a melting pot of cultures and often a battlefield.

In 15 BC the Romans set up a military camp called Vindobona, laying the foundations of what would become Vienna. Things moved swiftly in the 10th century when Vienna bloomed into one of the biggest towns north of the Alps under the Babenburg clan and commerce flourished. It rose to prominence in the 12th century as the seat of dukes and emperors. The city walls were completed in 1200, built on the ransom the English paid to release their imprisoned king, Richard the Lionheart.

The Habsburgs took power in 1278, beginning their 640-year reign. During medieval times, the city continued to prosper and the University of Vienna was founded in 1365. Developments came to a temporary halt when Ottoman forces invaded Austria and besieged Vienna in 1529, then again in 1683. Both attempts failed, and the Turks were defeated with Polish and German help.

Vienna boomed in the 17th and 18th centuries – palaces such as Prince Eugene of Savoy's Belvedere sprouted up, and the aristocracy poured pots of money into creating an impressive cityscape. Great minds like Mozart, Haydn, Beethoven and, in later years, Schubert and Strauss were drawn to the capital of classical music. But 1898 was marked by mourning when the country's beloved Empress Elisabeth (Sisi) was assassinated in Geneva.

In the wake of World War I, the Austro-Hungarian Empire collapsed in 1918. In 1938, Austria was annexed to Hitler's Germany and Vienna became a provincial capital in the Third Reich. The city's Jewish residents were forced into exile or murdered, and by the end of World War II in 1945 Vienna had been morally drained and physically devastated.

Austria became an EU member in 1995 and Vienna's historic centre was designated a UNESCO World Heritage Site in 2001. Having won admiration for hosting the Euro 2008 football finals, Vienna is very much on the up, as its top position in Mercer's Quality of Living Survey 2010 confirms. Things are set to get even better with the complete redevelopment of the Südbahnhof, giving Vienna a dazzling new central station to look forward to in 2014.

The Johann Strauss statue in the Stadtpark

Lifestyle

Traditional, trendy and everything in between, today's Vienna dishes up quite a few surprises. Yes, you'll find the parks and palaces basking in imperial splendour, but scratch the surface to unearth a growing crop of trendy lounge bars in Spittelberg, innovative boutiques in the MuseumsQuartier (see page 74) and a hot electronic music scene on the Danube Canal's banks. Skipping from Habsburg treasures to hedonism, and from old-style coffee houses to cocktails in glass-walled bars, Vienna is a master in the art of enjoyment.

The Viennese are a pleasure-seeking bunch, as the capital's knot of sleek boutiques, plush restaurants and chichi bars confirms. Great thinkers, dreamers and coffee drinkers, the laid-back locals love to relax and hate to rush. They even have a word to sum up this easy life – *Gemütlichkeit,* or snugness. Fit in by dwelling over an alfresco lunch, philosophising over a cup of coffee and watching the world go by in the Prater (see page 92). Unlike other capitals, this one simply doesn't do hectic.

Genuinely friendly when they come out of their formal shell, the Viennese are polite and happy to help. Most speak good English, although a smattering of German will go a long way if you're planning on exploring districts away from the centre. Life in Vienna revolves around having a good time, which could involve visiting an exhibition, going to a concert or taking a stroll in the woods. From Michelin-starred restaurants to picnicking in the park, this capital enjoys the high life but has its feet firmly on the ground – pretty but unpretentious, urban but with the countryside close at hand.

A lively student population of around 130,000 breathes new life into the city and makes sure it rocks by night. With a glut of cheery hostels around Mariahilfer Strasse, plus cheap-and-cheerful cafés and brewpubs clustering around the centre, a visit to Vienna doesn't have to cost a fortune. Seamlessly merging new and old, the capital has set out its 21st-century stall with a fresh, exciting take on art and shopping around the MuseumsQuartier, but has by no means lost sight of the value of its gloriously rich tradition.

Unwind over coffee at Café Central

Culture

Vienna has a burgeoning cultural scene. You won't have to search hard to immerse yourself in palatial museums crammed with masterpieces, inviting coffee houses where locals bury their heads in books and districts stacked with Baroque and Biedermeier houses. An intriguing mishmash of old and new, Vienna is a city where every corner transports you to another era.

In the city that inspired maestros like Beethoven, Mahler, Mozart, Schubert and Strauss, it's little wonder the Viennese take classical music seriously. The capital's greatest glory is the Staatsoper (Vienna State Opera, see page 66), staging some of the world's finest opera and ballet. Other big draws include chamber music at the Wiener Konzerthaus (see pages 95–6), the Vienna Philharmonic Orchestra and the **Volksoper** (ⓐ Währinger Str. 78 ⓣ 01 514 440 ⓦ www.volksoper.at) for musicals and operettas.

With 50 venues and a range of shows ranging from avant-garde plays to small-scale productions and cabaret, Vienna has a thriving theatre scene. Avid theatre-goers should try to get tickets for a performance at the 19th-century Burgtheater (see pages 63–4), which stages a variety of old favourites and new interpretations in an opulent setting, while the Volkstheater (see page 80) specialises in contemporary performances.

Unrivalled in the art department, Vienna is a kaleidoscope palette of Old Masters and new talent. Start off at the Hofburg (see page 58), which showcases glittering jewels and Biedermeier portraits, then head over to the Albertina (see page 63), with its clutch of Rembrandts, Picassos and Warhols, or gaze on the Kunsthistorisches Museum's riches (see page 64), which include works by Velázquez and Caravaggio. Design reaches a peak at the MAK Museum of Applied Arts (see page 66), which houses precious *Wiener Werkstätte* pieces. Visit the Upper Belvedere for great Impressionist works that really do make a great impression and a fine Klimt collection; or see Hundertwasser's colours make a Secessionist splash at KunstHaus Wien (see page 95).

KunstHaus Wien's unusual architecture

AFTER-DARK ARTS

Cultural vultures can get their after-dark fix when Vienna's museums stay open late once a week. After-hours art draws eventide aesthetes to establishments such as the Albertina (open until 21.00 on Wednesdays, see page 63), the MUMOK (Museum of Modern Art Ludwig Foundation, see page 79) and Leopold Museum (both open until 21.00 on Thursdays, see page 79), and the latest of them all, the MAK (open until 24.00 on Tuesdays, see page 66).

Adding a modern twist to Vienna's art offerings, the MuseumsQuartier (see page 74) is one of the ten largest cultural complexes in the world, spanning 45,000 sq m (54,000 sq yds). Take a trip to the cube-shaped Leopold Museum (see page 79), which houses an impressive collection of Egon Schiele paintings, or the Kunsthalle Wien (see pages 78–9), where contemporary art comes boldly to the fore.

The monolithic MUMOK (Museum of Modern Art Ludwig Foundation, see page 79) gives you an uncompromising shove into the 20th century with works by Warhol, Magritte and Kandinsky. For music and dance with a sharp cutting edge, look no further than Halle E & G (see page 78) and Tanzquartier Wien (see page 80).

The vibrant street scene around Stephansplatz

MAKING THE MOST OF
Vienna

Shopping

The savvy Viennese even came up with the idea of the coffee house to give shoppers' feet a break, and here that's just as well. The Austrian capital has some 20,000 shops, ranging from boho boutiques and Baroque antiques emporia to upmarket shopping centres. So whether you're after high fashion, dainty porcelain or a selection of chocolates to eat on the way home, you're in the right place.

Conveniently, the various forms of retail therapy can often be found in particular streets or areas. Designer labels dangle in the boutiques lining Kärntner Strasse, Graben and Kohlmarkt, where names like Armani and Tiffany & Co rub shoulders. On the streets fanning out from Stephansplatz, you'll find everything from the latest Viennese styles to confectionery and crystal. Look out for antiques on Dorotheergasse and Stallburggasse, or make for Mariahilfer Strasse for wall-to-wall high-street fashion.

Sometimes, of course, only the choice and convenience offered by a shopping centre will do. Find slinky shoes and cosmetics in the Ringstrassen Galerien (see page 68), or browse 50 shops under one roof at department store Steffl (see page 68) – take the glass elevator to the top for far-reaching views over Vienna. King of the malls, the giant **Gasometer** (ⓐ Guglgasse 14 ⓣ 01 743 64 30 ⓦ www.gasometer.at) in the 11th district houses big stores, snack bars and a 12-screen cinema.

Don't think for a minute that Vienna's shopping scene is staid or old-fashioned. A few steps from the Naschmarkt, Freihausviertel is packed with pocket-sized galleries and arty boutiques selling retro furniture, handmade ethnic jewellery

USEFUL SHOPPING PHRASES

What time do the shops open/close?
Um wieviel Uhr öffnen/schließen die Geschäfte?
Oom veefeel oor erffnen/shleessen dee geshefter?

How much is this?
Wieviel kostet das?
Veefeel kostet das?

Can I try this on?
Kann ich das anprobieren?
Can ikh das anprobeeren?

My size is ...
Ich habe Größe ...
Ikh haber grersser ...

I'll take this one, thank you
Ich nehme das, danke schön
Ikh neymer das, danker shern

This is too large/too small/too expensive
Es ist zu groß/zu klein/zu teuer
Es ist tsu gross/tsu kline/tsu toyer

and one-off artworks. For vintage fashion, ultra-modern gadgets and 60s psychedelia, head to Neubaugasse, Kirchengasse and the MuseumsQuartier's quartier21 (see page 74).

Shopping hours in the city are generally 09.00–18.30 Monday to Friday and 09.00–17.00 Saturday. Many shops stay open till 21.00 on Thursdays or Fridays. Souvenir shops, bakeries and station and airport shops open on Sundays.

When it comes to markets, there's an array of intriguing options. The pick of the bunch is Naschmarkt between the

Mariahilfer Strasse is the focal point for high-street shopping

4th and 6th districts, where stalls are piled high with fresh fruit, colourful spices, huge cheeses and barrels of glistening olives every single day from Monday to Friday, and second-hand finds are frequently going for a song at Saturday's flea market. There's also a plethora of cafés where you can join the locals for sushi or espresso. For fresh produce and a laid-back feel, make for Karmelitermarkt and Rochusmarkt (see page 96).

If you're interested in taking home a souvenir of your trip, go for some Augarten porcelain (well wrapped, of course!), multicoloured Hundertwasser postcards, a hand-painted Lipizzaner stallion to decorate your own palace and some candied violets from Demel for a lingering taste of Vienna.

Eating & drinking

Vienna serves fine food at far more affordable prices than many other European capitals. There are thousands of places to eat, including sleek tapas and sushi bars, elegant Michelin-starred restaurants and the ubiquitous *würstelstände* (sausage stands). Whether it's to be a cavernous brewpub with homebrews and tasty snacks or a wood-panelled wine tavern, this city defies anyone to go hungry.

When it comes to dining districts, the centre's eateries are a mouthwatering fusion of Viennese classics and world flavours. Tucked down the streets fanning out from Stephansplatz are relaxed taverns and gourmet haunts, ultra-modern sushi bars and snug coffee houses serving tasty and often inexpensive fare. Venture into the city's less touristy districts to mingle with the locals and sample authentic snacks. If you like to dine with a view there are some great places around the MuseumsQuartier (see page 74) where you can eat surrounded by striking architecture. For alfresco dining and people-watching, you should head for the laid-back cafés and restaurants around the Prater and Donauinsel.

PRICE CATEGORIES
The restaurant price guides used in this book indicate the approximate cost of a three-course meal for one person, excluding drinks.
£ up to €20 **££** €20–40 **£££** over €40

Markets are the place to stock up on your own food. In the Wieden district, Vienna's vibrant Naschmarkt (see pages 23–4) is an attraction in its own right. Alongside the mounds of fresh fruit are huge cheeses, seafood, olives and racks of colourful spices. You can spend hours wandering from stall to stall, popping into cafés for an espresso and eating your way around the world at hole-in-the-wall restaurants dishing up everything from falafel and curries to sushi and sizzling stir-fries fresh from the wok.

Vienna's manicured gardens and shady parks are the ideal place for a picnic when the sun shines. Fill your basket with local specialities and head for the Volksgarten (see page 63) to rest beside the fountains and roses, or lay your blanket down by the water's edge on the Danube Island (see page 34).

A melting pot of Austrian, Bohemian, Hungarian and Balkan flavours, Viennese cuisine encompasses flavoursome and hearty

The area around Naschmarkt is full of cafés and restaurants

USEFUL DINING PHRASES

I would like a table for ... people, please
Ein Tisch für ... Personen, bitte
Ine tish foor ... perzohnen, bitter

Waiter/waitress!
Herr Ober/Frau Kellnerin!
Hair ohber/frow kell-nair-in!

May I have the bill, please?
Die Rechnung, bitte.
Dee rekhnung, bitter.

I am a vegetarian. Does this contain meat?
Ich bin Vegetarier (Vegetarierin *fem.*).
Enthält das hier Fleisch?
Ikh bin veggetaareer (veggetaareerin).
Enthelt dass heer flyshe?

Where is the toilet (restroom) please?
Wo sind die Toiletten, bitte?
Voo zeent dee toletten, bitter?

I would like a cup of/two cups of/another coffee/tea, please
Ich hätte gern eine Tasse/zwei Tassen/noch eine Tasse Kaffee/Tee, bitte
Ikh hett-er gairn iner tasser/tsvy tassen/nok iner tasser kafey/tey, bitter

I would like a beer/two beers, please
Ich hätte gern ein Bier/zwei Bier, bitte
Ikh hett-er gairn ine beer/tsvy beer, bitter

COFFEE CULTURE

A far cry from the quick caffeine fix, Vienna likes to linger and savour coffee at its leisure. From old-world giants like Sacher (see page 69), decked out with chandeliers, to shabby-chic cafés with creaking floors, the Viennese coffee house is an institution where locals come to chat, philosophise, write, read the daily papers and enjoy concerts.

Some coffee houses feature 20 different varieties, including *Grosse Schwarzer* (double espresso), *Fiaker* (strong black coffee laced with kirsch and topped with whipped cream and a cherry) and *Maria Theresia* (mocha with orange liqueur and whipped cream).

local specialities. Traditional fare includes *Wiener Schnitzel* (breaded veal cutlet), Hungarian-style *Fiakergulasch* (beef goulash with plenty of paprika), *Klare Rindsuppe* (beef broth) with *Griessknockerl* (semolina dumplings) and *Tafelspitz* (braised beef). Try the home-grown Riesling and Grüner Veltiner wines, or sample local beers like 7 Stern Bräu and Salm Bräu in brewery pubs. The sweet-toothed Viennese always save a bit of room for dessert. Leave the calorie counter at home and take the opportunity to tuck into flaky apple strudel, *Kaiserschmarren* (sugared pancakes with raisins) and *Powidltaschen* (potato puffs filled with plum jam).

Many venues include a service charge in the bill, but it's normal to leave a tip if you were pleased with the service. Locals usually tip around five to ten per cent. Do this when you pay the bill rather than leaving money on the table.

Entertainment & nightlife

Vienna positively twinkles by night, as the Hofburg (see page 58) shines and the capital's bars and restaurants glow. Whether you're looking for a relaxed pub in which to chill out or a sleek lounge bar to hang out with a young, fashionable crowd or dance until dawn, this 24-hour city will not disappoint.

Vienna's nightlife changes with the seasons. Summer here spells late nights in lounge bars and chestnut-tree-shaded gardens, where night owls spill out on to pocket-sized terraces and inner courtyards. As the nights get colder, the Viennese head indoors and fend off cool weather by sipping fruity Rieslings in cosy *Heurige* and unwinding in wood-panelled cafés with old-world musty charm.

There are few cities in the world that can match Vienna when it comes to culture (see page 18). The capital steps light-footedly from opera to classical music, theatre, live jazz and cabaret. If you have the time, try to sample a little bit of each. To book tickets in advance, contact the particular venue direct or try **Vienna Ticket Office** (ⓐ Kärntner Str. 51 ⓣ 01 513 11 11 ⓦ www.viennaticketoffice.com), which covers major festivals, gigs and performances.

WHAT'S ON?

Hauptstadt (ⓦ www.hauptstadt.at) gives the lowdown on Vienna's nightlife, including clubs, concerts, cinema and cabaret, while online magazine *Falter* (ⓦ www.falter.at) has the latest listings (both in German).

A VINE TIME

Keep an eye out for Vienna's *Heurigen,* traditional taverns serving only locally produced wines together with tasty buffet snacks and occasionally Austrian folk music. You'll know you've found one of these quintessential Viennese haunts when you see a sprig of pine branches above the door and a sign saying *Ausg'steckt,* which means it's open for custom. Most wine taverns lie on the city's fringes in the 16th, 19th and 21st districts. Come to taste the grape and drink in the laid-back atmosphere.

Within the Ring, the so-called 'Bermuda Triangle' has a glut of upbeat bars, cafés and clubs vying for your custom and inviting a lengthy bar crawl. The centre's main drag, this is the go-to district for wall-to-wall entertainment, music and an image-conscious crowd that comes to see and be seen. But it's not all preening and posing. One of the top addresses to seek out is Krah Krah (see page 73), where you'll find brilliant beers and an atmosphere of back-slapping bonhomie.

Tuned into emerging trends and tastes, Vienna has a vibrant alternative pulse that beats around the über-cool Gürtel area, where you can party to urban and electro beats in bars with an industrial edge beneath the railway arches. When you tire of the pulsating bass, make for nearby Spittelberg, where creaking pubs, chichi cocktail lounges and vibrant bars huddle in a web of narrow streets.

Clubbers dance till dawn by the Danube, and the Prater (see page 92) peps up the late-night scene to keep partygoers on their toes. In the central part of the city, the beautiful people share the dance floor at Volksgarten (see page 73) overlooking the Imperial Palace, while DJs keep dance floors rammed, spinning drum'n'bass, electro and techno at Flex (see page 73).

As night falls, Vienna's stages light up. Book tickets well ahead to catch world-class contemporary and classic performances at the sumptuous Burgtheater (National Theatre, see pages 63–4), and opera, ballet and classical music at the grand 19th-century Staatsoper (Vienna State Opera, see page 66). If you want something a bit less mainstream, the MuseumsQuartier's Halle E & G (see page 78) and Tanzquartier Wien (see page 80) are at the crest of cutting-edge performing arts.

A super-stylish bar at the Spittelberg (see page 74)

Sport & relaxation

SPECTATOR SPORTS

Football

Footy fans should try to catch a match at the state-of-the-art Ernst-Happel-Stadion, Austria's largest stadium and home to the national football team. ⓐ Meiereistr. 7 ⓣ 01 728 08 54 ⓦ U-Bahn: U2 Stadion

PARTICIPATION SPORTS

Bungee jumping

Daredevils dangle upside-down from the 152-m (499-ft) Danube Tower. The world's highest jump from a tower, this nerve-splintering experience is available from April to early November. ⓐ Donauturmstr. 4 ⓣ 01 263 35 72 ⓦ www.donauturm.at ⓦ Bus: 20B Danube Tower

Swimming

In summer, locals cool off with a dip in the open-air Badeschiff barge on the Danube Canal, featuring a 30-m (98-ft) swimming pool. ⓐ Donaukanal ⓣ 01 513 07 44 ⓦ www.badeschiff.at ⓦ U-Bahn: U1 Schwedenplatz ❗ Admission charge

GET YOUR SKATES ON!

Vienna gets ready to roll at 21.00 every Friday from May to September, as skaters gather at Heldenplatz to flit through the city's streets. To join this fun, free whirlwind tour of the sights by night, check out ⓦ www.nightskating.at

Rollerblading is a popular pastime in Vienna

Walking & cycling

Dappled with expansive parks and gardens, Vienna is a terrific city for walking and cycling. Wander the leafy Prater and the Belvedere's alpine gardens, or hop on a bike to explore the marked trails which crisscross the nearby Wienerwald.

RELAXATION

Hammam

Pamper yourself by getting all steamed up in this delightful, oriental-style hammam which is only a stone's throw away from the MuseumsQuartier. Ⓐ Rahlgasse 5 Ⓣ 01 585 66 45 Ⓦ www.auxgazelles.at Ⓛ 12.00–22.00 Mon–Sat, closed Sun Ⓝ U-Bahn: U2 MuseumsQuartier Ⓘ Admission charge

Leisure

Water is never far away in Vienna. When the weather gets warm, the Danube Island attracts crowds to its bays, tree-fringed promenade and waterfront cafés. You can come to this major chill-out zone to swim, stroll, skate or even hire a boat. There's even a naturist area for those who dare to bare!

Ⓝ U-Bahn: U1 Donauinsel

Spa

Unwind in Oberlaa's cascading thermal baths with waters that bubble up around 36°C (97°F), pummelling massage points and a Feng Shui-inspired sauna complex. Ⓐ Kurbadstr. 14 Ⓣ 01 680 09 96 00 Ⓦ www.oberlaa.at Ⓛ 08.45–22.00 Mon–Sat, 07.45–22.00 Sun Ⓝ U-Bahn: U1 Reumannplatz; Tram: 67 Ⓘ Admission charge

Accommodation

From cheap-and-cheerful backpacker digs with a 24-hour party vibe to neat-and-petite guesthouses with bags of charm, Vienna has something to suit every style and pocket.

HOTELS

Hotel Praterstern £ A smartly decorated hotel near the Prater that offers excellent value. The wood-floored rooms in crisp whites and blues have Internet access. Unwind in the tranquil garden. ⓐ Mayergasse 6 (Leopoldstadt & Landstrasse) ⓣ 01 214 01 23 ⓦ www.hotelpraterstern.at U-Bahn: U1 Praterstern

Hotel Kugel ££ This turn-of-the-century hotel has rooms with individual flair, all with satellite TV and many with canopy beds and minibars. The friendly staff will help you plan your stay. Prices include a buffet breakfast. ⓐ Siebensterngasse 43 (Neubau) ⓣ 01 523 33 55 ⓦ www.hotelkugel.at U-Bahn: U3 Neubaugasse

Hotel Urania ££ Pick a room to match your personality at Vienna's quirkiest hotel. Each room has a theme – from Baroque frescoes and Japanese minimalism to medieval chambers and wood-

PRICE CATEGORIES

The ratings below indicate the approximate cost of a room for two people for one night.

£ up to €65 **££** €65–100 **£££** over €120

panelled alpine chalet designs. ⓐ Obere Weissgerberstr. 7 (Leopoldstadt & Landstrasse) ⓣ 01 713 17 11 ⓦ www.hotel-urania.at ⓢ U-Bahn: U1 Schwedenplatz

Do & Co £££ The final word in urban chic, this design hotel has perhaps the best location in Vienna: housed in the Haas Haus on Stephansplatz overlooking St Stephan's Cathedral. Rooms recall stylish NYC apartments with their hardwood floors, glass-walled bathrooms and DVD players. Go up to the lounge bar or rooftop for panoramic city views. ⓐ Stephansplatz 12 (City Centre) ⓣ 01 24 188 ⓦ www.doco.com ⓢ U-Bahn: U1 Stephansplatz

Grand Hotel Wien £££ The belle époque Grand Hotel has luxurious rooms and suites, two top-notch restaurants and a traditional café, all within a couple of minutes' walk of the Opera House. ⓐ Kärntner Ring 9 (City Centre) ⓣ 01 515 800 ⓦ www.grandhotel.com ⓢ U-Bahn: U4 Oper

Hotel Rathaus Wein & Design £££ Everything at this sleek concept hotel revolves around wine – from wine cosmetics to wine cheese at breakfast. Minimalist chic sums up the Zen-inspired rooms and the all-important touches are there – from free welcome baskets to wine tasting. ⓐ Lange Gasse 13 (City Centre) ⓣ 01 400 11 22 ⓦ www.hotel-rathaus-wien.at ⓢ U-Bahn: U3 Volkstheater

GUESTHOUSES

K&T Boarding House £ Right in the thick of things on Mariahilfer Strasse, this family-run place is a terrific budget find.

The high-ceilinged rooms are bright and spacious and have kettles. There's no breakfast, but you'll find plenty of bakeries nearby. Ⓐ Mariahilfer Strasse 72 (Neubau) Ⓣ 01 523 29 89 Ⓦ www.ktboardinghouse.at Ⓝ U-Bahn: U3 Neubaugasse

Wallow in 5-star luxury at the Grand Hotel Wien

Pension Hargita £ Expect a warm welcome at this 2-star Neubau guesthouse. The squeaky clean, light-filled rooms are decked out in cheery yellows and blues. ⓐ Andreasgasse 1/8 (Neubau) ⓣ 01 526 19 28 ⓦ www.hargita.at ⓝ U-Bahn: U3 Zieglergasse

Pension Kraml £ Close to Mariahilfer Strasse, this elegant 19th-century town house set around a courtyard scores points for its large, quiet rooms and substantial buffet breakfast. The comfy rooms in earthy tones have wood floors, huge windows and all mod cons. ⓐ Brauergasse 5 (Neubau) ⓣ 01 587 85 88 ⓦ www.pensionkraml.at ⓝ U-Bahn: U3 Zieglergasse

Pharmador £ An intimate guesthouse set round a pretty courtyard, Pharmador offers spacious, comfortable rooms with satellite TV, minibar and free wireless Internet access. Guests enjoy free parking and a buffet breakfast with fresh produce. ⓐ Schottenfeldgasse 39 (Neubau) ⓣ 01 523 53 17 ⓦ www.pensionpharmador.at ⓝ U-Bahn: U6 Burggasse/Stadthalle

Stadtnest ££ Charming B&B in a late 19th-century town house in the 6th district. Rooms are large and well appointed, there's free Internet access and rates include a delicious breakfast with organic and home-made produce. ⓐ Stumpergasse 29 (Neubau) ⓣ 01 545 49 38 ⓦ www.stadtnest.at ⓝ U-Bahn: U3 Zieglergasse

Suzanne ££ The rooms at this 19th-century guesthouse offer a touch of old-world grandeur with their high ceilings, antique furniture and chandeliers. ⓐ Walfischgasse 4 (City Centre)

01 513 25 07 www.pension-suzanne.at U-Bahn: U1/U4 Karlsplatz/Oper

HOSTELS

Hostel Ruthensteiner £ A family affair, this cosy hostel three minutes' walk from Westbahnhof has a leafy courtyard, barbecue area, communal kitchen, free lockers and high-speed Internet access. Robert Hamerlinggasse 24 (Neubau) 01 893 42 02 www.hostelruthensteiner.com U-Bahn: U3/U6 Westbahnhof

Wombat's City Hostel 'The Lounge' £ Voted the world's cleanest hostel, dorms come with shower, free welcome drink, breakfast buffet, lockers, laundry, kitchen and Internet access. Party in the womBar. Mariahilfer Str. 137 (Neubau) 01 897 23 36 www.wombats-hostels.com U-Bahn: U3, U6 Westbahnhof

CAMPSITES

Aktiv Camping Neue Donau £ Peaceful site near the Prater. Facilities include a shop, barbecue area, Internet access and bike rental. Am Kleehäufel (Leopoldstadt & Landstrasse) 01 202 40 10 www.wiencamping.at Apr–Sept U-Bahn: U1 Kaisermühlen; Bus: 91A

Camping Wien Süd £ This family-friendly site near Lake Brunn is surrounded by woods and meadows, with barbecue area, playground and communal kitchen. Breitenfurter Str. 269 (Leopoldstadt & Landstrasse) 01 867 36 49 www.wiencamping.at June–Aug U-Bahn: U6 Am Schöpfwerk; Bus: 62A

THE BEST OF VIENNA

Time your visit with waltz-like precision to make the most of Vienna's cultural attractions, happening bars and fine dining. You can't see it all in one visit – and you'll surely be back for more.

TOP 10 ATTRACTIONS

- **Hofburg (Imperial Palace)** Admire the lavish state apartments and some seriously glittering crown jewels at this vast palace complex, which was once home to the Austrian Habsburgs (see page 58).

- **MuseumsQuartier** Explore one of the ten biggest cultural districts in the world, full of avant-garde architecture, modern art and funky boutiques (see pages 74–87).

- **Prater** The big wheel turns, carousels tinkle and roller coasters offer eye-popping thrills at this massive funfair set in acres of parkland (see page 92).

- **Stephansdom (St Stephen's Cathedral)** Gaze up at the filigree spires and mosaic roof of Vienna's Gothic cathedral and climb to the top for giddy views (see page 62).

Suggested itineraries

HALF-DAY: VIENNA IN A HURRY

Whizz around the Ring on a tram to spot highlights including the Rathaus (City Hall, see page 59) and Staatsoper (State Opera, see page 66). Pause at the Hofburg palace (see page 58) to take a peek at the sumptuous state apartments, then scale the tower of Stephansdom (St Stephen's Cathedral, see page 62) for sweeping views over Vienna's rooftops.

Mares and their brood at the Spanische Hofreitschule

1 DAY: TIME TO SEE A LITTLE MORE

Make a beeline for the MuseumsQuartier to seek out Klimt masterpieces in the Leopold Museum (see page 79) and quirky gifts in quartier21 (see page 74). Nip over to Spittelberg (see page 74) for an alfresco lunch on the cobblestones. Get your cultural fix with Rembrandt and Warhol originals in the splendid Albertina (see page 63).

2–3 DAYS: TIME TO SEE MUCH MORE

See Lipizzaner stallions perform at the Spanische Hofreitschule (Spanish Riding School, see page 62) and head to Leopoldstadt to stand in awe of the crazed colours of Hundertwasserhaus (see page 89). By night enjoy theatrical highs at the illuminated Burgtheater (National Theatre, see pages 63–4). Rent a bike to cycle trails weaving through the Prater (stopping for a ride on the iconic Ferris wheel, see page 92). Before you return, pick up gifts from the high-street stores lining Mariahilfer Strasse.

LONGER: ENJOYING VIENNA TO THE FULL

If time isn't a problem, stay longer to discover the region's rich pickings. Go west to the Wienerwald to see Seegrotte Hinterbrühl (Europe's largest subterranean lake, see pages 109–10), glimpse precipitous gorges and hill walk in tranquil nature reserves. Climb Leopold-Figl-Warte (see page 109) for some spectacular alpine views.

An hour's drive from Vienna, the River Danube snakes through the Wachau Valley (see pages 115–24). This UNESCO World Heritage Site has a clutch of Benedictine abbeys, cliff-top castles and gently sloping vineyards.

Something for nothing

The good news for those on a budget is that plenty of Vienna's sights can be enjoyed for free. Kick off your stay with a poke through the biggest and most vibrant food market, the Naschmarkt (see pages 23–4), to immerse yourself in local flavour. Swap the grand concert halls for street entertainment in the shadow of Stephansdom (see page 62), where first-rate puppeteers, musicians and opera singers give the pros a run for their money.

Chilling out in the Prater costs nothing

FREE FESTIVALS

Spring and summer step up a gear with a host of free festivals. The pick of the bunch are the City Festival (May) with theatre, concerts and late-night parties, the cultural highs of the Vienna Festival (mid-May–mid-June) and the open-air concerts at the Danube Island Festival (June).

For the cost of a tram ticket, you can arrange your personalised tour of the sights on the Ring – take tram lines 1 or 2 for fleeting glimpses of the immense Hofburg (see page 58) and Rathaus (see page 59). Pause to admire the Volksgarten's attractive fountains, flowers and sculptures (see page 63). Stepping over to Landstrasse, you don't have to be a dedicated art lover to be enthralled by the Hundertwasserhaus (see page 89), an amazingly vibrant explosion of colour and mosaics that doesn't cost a penny to admire.

You can easily spend an afternoon combing the hip Spittelberg district's warren of cobbled streets, punctuated with beautiful Biedermeier town houses, art studios and pavement cafés.

Nature costs nothing in the University of Vienna Botanical Gardens (see page 93), where you can spot alpine species, tropical ferns and Antarctic beech trees. Join the locals to stroll through the shady Prater (see page 92) on a Sunday morning or hang out with the Viennese and soak up some rays on the Donauinsel (Danube Island, see page 34). On the city's fringes, visit the Lainzer Tiergarten (see page 109) with its peaceful oak woods, where you can spy red deer, wild boar and woodpeckers.

When it rains

With an abundance of indoor sights, museums and shops, there's no need to let sudden downpours put a dampener on your stay in Vienna. Head for the city's shopping malls and galleries, snuggle up in a *Heurige* wine cellar to taste local wines, or warm up Viennese-style in one of the gorgeous coffee houses.

Serving delicious cakes, free newspapers and a dollop of culture, the capital's cafés help you forget the wet weather. Sip a frothy melange coffee beneath vaulted ceilings in elegant Central (see page 69), browse magazines in wood-panelled

SCHÖNBRUNN PALACE

Allow a day to take in this magnificent UNESCO World Heritage Site, once Empress Sisi's Baroque summer residence. It's one of the most important cultural monuments in Austria, with its palace, park and zoo (see page 130) visited by some 6.7 million people a year. Feel the heat of the tropics in the 20-m (66-ft) high Palm House and view the Hall of Mirrors where Mozart once played. The Imperial Coach Collection gleams with golden carriages and the Millions Room has magnificent rosewood panelling. There are tours around the Imperial apartments.

ⓐ Schönbrunner Schlossstr. 47–49 (Hietzing) ⓣ 01 811 130 ⓦ www.schoenbrunn.at ⓛ 08.30–16.30 (winter); 08.30–18.00 (summer) U-Bahn: U4 Schönbrunn ! Admission charge

While away a rainy day at the iconic Hotel Sacher

Sperl (see page 85), or visit the celebrated Sacher (see page 69) for a slice of rich chocolatey *Sachertorte*.

When the heavens open, the locals love to shop. Join them in the central Steffl department store (see page 68) and the smart Ringstrassen Galerien mall (see page 68).

The city's galleries are an obvious choice when rain sets in. Take shelter in the Belvedere Gallery (see page 95), which has everything from Klimt paintings to medieval masterpieces, or go to the KunstHaus Wien (see page 95), with its wonderful Hundertwasser works hung on irregular walls. And don't forget the MuseumsQuartier, with attractions including Architekturzentrum Wien (see page 78), the Kunsthalle Wien (see pages 78–9), the Leopold Museum (see page 79), MUMOK (see page 79) and the ZOOM Kindermuseum (see page 81).

On arrival

TIME DIFFERENCE

Like the rest of Austria, Vienna is on Central European Time (CET), an hour ahead of Greenwich Mean Time (GMT) in winter and British Summer Time (late Mar–end Oct).

ARRIVING

By air

Situated 20 km (12 miles) from the centre, **Vienna International Airport** (t 01 70070 w www.viennaairport.com) serves European destinations including London, Paris and Berlin. No-frills airlines offering cheap flights include easyJet, Germanwings and Air Berlin. The user-friendly airport has services including ATMs, shops, currency exchange and cafés. Departing every 30 minutes from 05.30 to 23.00, the City Airport Train whisks you to central Vienna (Landstrasse/Wien Mitte) in 16 minutes (about €18 return). A taxi into town costs around €35.

A budget alternative is to travel with Ryanair from London Stansted or Dublin to Bratislava in Slovakia, 80 km (50 miles) from Vienna. For details, see w www.airportbratislava.sk

By rail

The Südbahnhof is undergoing complete renovation to become Vienna's central station by 2014. In the meantime, most national and international trains arrive at Vienna's Westbahnhof (a Europaplatz U U-Bahn: U3, U6) in Vienna's 15th district, which has newsagents, cafés and a post office. Regional and local trains arrive at stations including Franz-Josefs-Bahnhof

IF YOU GET LOST, TRY ...

Excuse me, do you speak English?
Entschuldigen Sie, sprechen Sie Englisch?
Entshuldigen zee, shprekhen zee english?

Excuse me, is this the right way to the city centre/ the tourist office/the station/the bus station?
Entschuldigung, geht es hier zur Stadtmitte/zur Touristeninformation/zum Bahnhof/zum Busbahnhof?
Entshuldeegoong, gayt es here tsoor shtatmitter/tsoor touristeninformatsiown/tsoom baanhof/tsoom busbaanhof?

Can you point to it on my map, please?
Können Sie es mir bitte auf der Karte zeigen?
Kernen see es meer bitter owf der kaarte tsygen?

(S-Bahn: S40) and Wien Mitte (U-Bahn: U3/U4). Austria's national rail network **ÖBB** (www.oebb.at) runs an efficient service to major cities including Salzburg, Innsbruck and Linz, plus international destinations like Berlin, Paris, Munich, Basel and Bratislava.

By road

Most international and long-distance buses pull into several locations across the city including Landstrasse/Wien Mitte and Schwedenplatz. Eurolines and National Express operate a frequent service. 01 711 01 (bus information)

POI
Motorway
Main Road
Minor Road
Airport
Railway
Prague & Stockerau
Korneuburg
A22
Klosterneuburg
Döbling
Donau-park
Währing
Leopoldstadt
Untermauerbach
Hernals
VIENNA
Hadersdorf
Ottakring
Purkersdorf
Penzing
Landstrasse
A1
Lainzer Tiergarten
A23
Hietzing
St Pölten and Linz
Hermesvilla
Favoriten
Mauer
Kalksburg
Liesing
A2
Perchtoldsdorf
Weiner Neustadt & Graz

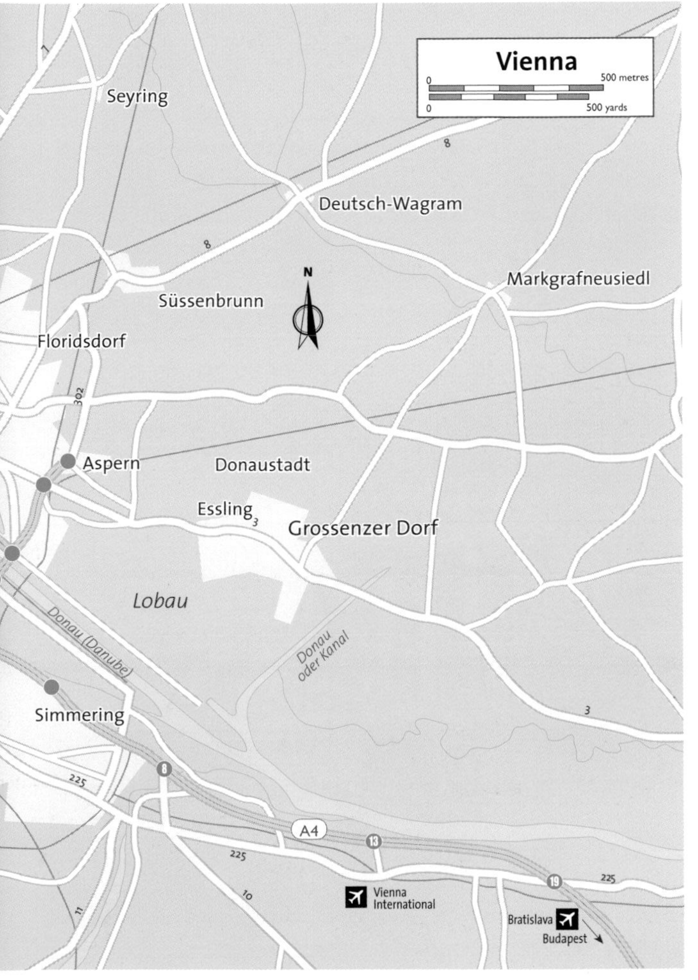

Vienna
0
500 metres
0
500 yards
Seyring
Deutsch-Wagram
Markgrafneusiedl
Süssenbrunn
N
Floridsdorf
Aspern
Donaustadt
Essling
Grossenzer Dorf
Lobau
Donau (Danube)
Donau oder Kanal
Simmering
A4
Vienna International
Bratislava
Budapest

Vienna is well connected to the rest of Austria and Europe via the A1, A2 and A4 Autobahns. To drive on Austria's motorways, it's a legal requirement that you display a *Vignette* (toll sticker) in the front windscreen, which you can buy at the airport or in petrol stations. Short-stay parking is available in central Vienna (districts 1 to 9 and 20) – you'll need a valid *Parkschein* (parking ticket) which you can buy from most newsagents. Some hotels can arrange an all-day parking permit. The city's good-value, easily accessible P+R garages (ⓦ www.parkandride.at) are better for longer stays.

Trams are a speedy way to get around the Ring

FINDING YOUR FEET

Vienna is generally a safe city and the crime rate is low. It's unlikely you'll experience any problems during your stay, but it's wise to exercise caution if walking in dimly lit, less-populated areas at night. Pickpockets sometimes target travellers in crowded areas of the city, so be aware of where you have your handbag or wallet.

ORIENTATION

The city splits into 23 districts (*Bezirke*), each with its own flavour and attractions. Many sights including the Hofburg and St Stephen's Cathedral cluster in the historic centre (*Innere Stadt*) encircled by the 4-km (½-mile) Ringstrasse, a wide boulevard often simply called the Ring. Districts 1 to 9 represent the city centre (*Innenbezirke*) and spider out to Vienna's outer districts (*Außenbezirke*).

Heading west you reach the MuseumsQuartier in Neubau, while Leopoldstadt and Landstrasse to the east are home to the Hundertwasserhaus and Prater Park's enormous Ferris wheel. Schönbrunn Palace (see page 46) is situated 4.5 km (3 miles) south of the centre in Hietzing.

GETTING AROUND

An efficient public transport network makes getting around easy. If you're planning on making more than one trip, save by buying a 24-hour pass for around €6 or a 72-hour network pass for about €14, which offers unlimited use of the city's trams, buses and U-Bahn (metro). Remember to stamp your ticket the first time you travel. **Wiener Linien** (w www.wienerlinien.at) provides detailed maps and timetables. Operating from 06.00

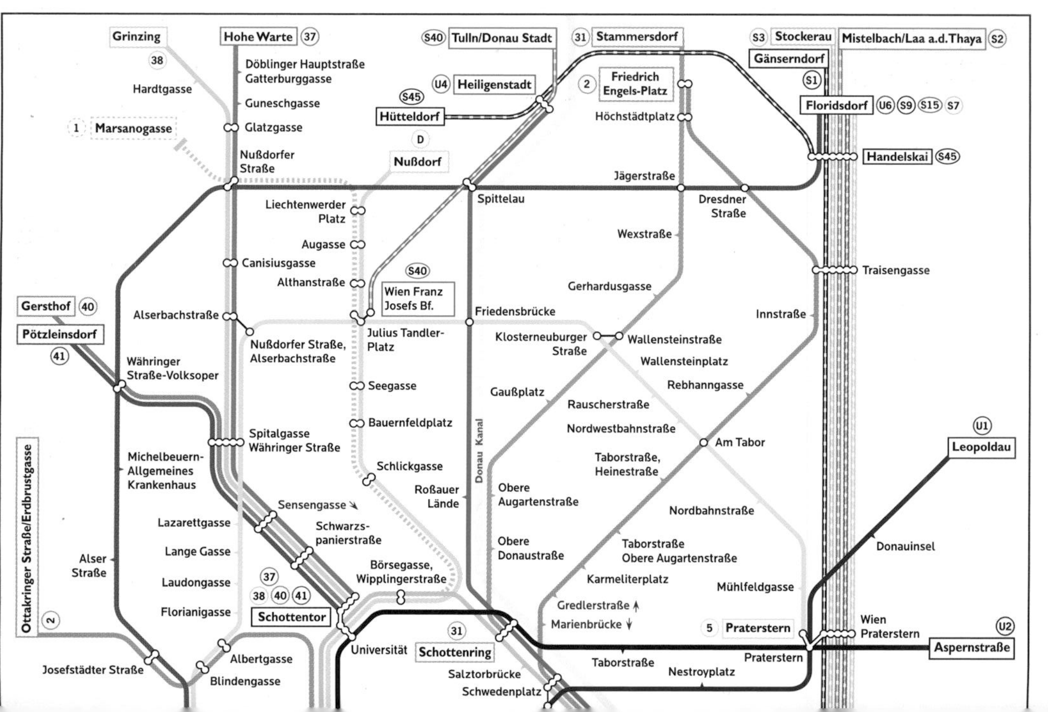

Grinzing 38
Hohe Warte 37
S40 Tulln/Donau Stadt
31 Stammersdorf
S3 Stockerau
Mistelbach/Laa a.d.Thaya S2
Gänserndorf
S1
Floridsdorf U6 S9 S15 S7
Handelskai S45
Döblinger Hauptstraße
Gatterburggasse
Hardtgasse
Guneschgasse
U4 Heiligenstadt
S45 Hütteldorf
2 Friedrich Engels-Platz
Höchstädtplatz
1 Marsanogasse
Glatzgasse
D Nußdorf
Nußdorfer Straße
Jägerstraße
Spittelau
Dresdner Straße
Liechtenwerder Platz
Wexstraße
Augasse
Canisiusgasse
S40 Wien Franz Josefs Bf.
Althanstraße
Traisengasse
Gerhardusgasse
Gersthof 40
Pötzleinsdorf 41
Alserbachstraße
Friedensbrücke
Innstraße
Julius Tandler-Platz
Nußdorfer Straße, Alserbachstraße
Klosterneuburger Straße
Wallensteinstraße
Währinger Straße-Volksoper
Wallensteinplatz
Seegasse
Gaußplatz
Rebhanngasse
Rauscherstraße
Bauernfeldplatz
Spitalgasse Währinger Straße
Nordwestbahnstraße
Am Tabor
U1 Leopoldau
Donau Kanal
Michelbeuern-Allgemeines Krankenhaus
Schlickgasse
Taborstraße, Heinestraße
Roßauer Lände
Obere Augartenstraße
Sensengasse
Nordbahnstraße
Lazarettgasse
Schwarzspanierstraße
Ottakringer Straße/Erdbrustgasse
Donauinsel
Lange Gasse
Taborstraße Obere Augartenstraße
Obere Donaustraße
Alser Straße
Börsegasse, Wipplingerstraße
Laudongasse
Karmeliterplatz
Mühlfeldgasse
37 38 40 41 Schottentor
Gredlerstraße
Florianigasse
Marienbrücke
Wien Praterstern
2
5 Praterstern
U2 Aspernstraße
Universität
31 Schottenring
Albertgasse
Praterstern
Taborstraße
Josefstädter Straße
Salztorbrücke
Nestroyplatz
Blindengasse
Schwedenplatz

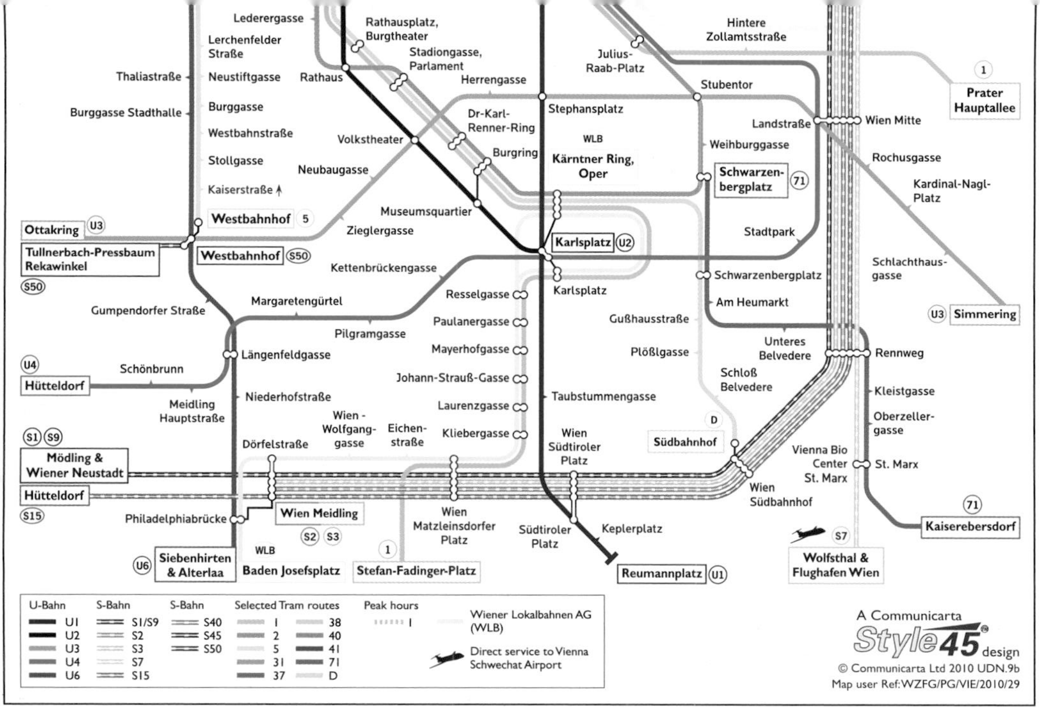

Lederergasse
Lerchenfelder Straße
Thaliastraße
Neustiftgasse
Burggasse Stadthalle
Burggasse
Westbahnstraße
Stollgasse
Kaiserstraße
Ottakring (U3)
Westbahnhof (5)
Tullnerbach-Pressbaum Rekawinkel (S50)
Westbahnhof (S50)
Rathausplatz, Burgtheater
Rathaus
Stadiongasse, Parlament
Herrengasse
Volkstheater
Neubaugasse
Dr-Karl-Renner-Ring
Burgring
Museumsquartier
Zieglergasse
Kettenbrückengasse
Gumpendorfer Straße
Margaretengürtel
Pilgramgasse
Längenfeldgasse
(U4) Hütteldorf
Schönbrunn
Meidling Hauptstraße
Niederhofstraße
(S1) (S9) Mödling & Wiener Neustadt
Hütteldorf (S15)
Dörfelstraße
Wien - Wolfgang-gasse
Eichen-straße
Philadelphiabrücke
Wien Meidling (S2) (S3)
WLB
Baden Josefsplatz
(U6) Siebenhirten & Alterlaa
Stefan-Fadinger-Platz (1)
Wien Matzleinsdorfer Platz
Resselgasse
Paulanergasse
Mayerhofgasse
Johann-Strauß-Gasse
Laurenzgasse
Kliebergasse
Stephansplatz
WLB
Kärntner Ring, Oper
Karlsplatz (U2)
Karlsplatz
Taubstummengasse
Wien Südtiroler Platz
Südtiroler Platz
Keplerplatz
Reumannplatz (U1)
Julius-Raab-Platz
Hintere Zollamtsstraße
Stubentor
Landstraße
Wien Mitte
Weihburggasse
Schwarzenbergplatz (71)
Stadtpark
Schwarzenbergplatz
Am Heumarkt
Gußhausstraße
Plößlgasse
Unteres Belvedere
Schloß Belvedere
Südbahnhof (D)
Wien Südbahnhof
Vienna Bio Center St. Marx
Prater Hauptallee (1)
Rochusgasse
Kardinal-Nagl-Platz
Schlachthaus-gasse
(U3) Simmering
Rennweg
Kleistgasse
Oberzeller-gasse
St. Marx
Kaiserebersdorf (71)
Wolfsthal & Flughafen Wien (S7)

U-Bahn	S-Bahn	S-Bahn	Selected Tram routes		Peak hours	
U1	S1/S9	S40	1	38	I	Wiener Lokalbahnen AG (WLB)
U2	S2	S45	2	40		Direct service to Vienna Schwechat Airport
U3	S3	S50	5	41		
U4	S7		31	71		
U6	S15		37	D		

A Communicarta Style45® design

Map user Ref: WZFG/PG/VIE/2010/29

to 24.00 daily, the speedy U-Bahn metro system features five lines that criss-cross the city and travel to the suburbs: U1, U2, U3, U4 and U6 (there is no U5).

Vienna's red-and-white trams are a scenic way of getting about town. Trams run every five to ten minutes from 06.00 to 24.00 and you'll find timetables at every stop. Around 80 bus lines streak the city and night buses operate along the main routes every 30 minutes until 05.00. Sightseeing buses (see ⓦ www.viennasightseeing.at) offer guided tours and allow you to hop on and off as you please.

Taxis operate on a meter (and do note that there's a surcharge for luggage and for all trips after 23.00), but, to avoid any financial shocks, negotiate the fare first if you want to travel to the city's suburbs; this should not be too difficult since most taxi drivers speak reasonable English. Those of the tipping persuasion can reward the driver to the tune of five to ten per cent of the fare.

CAR HIRE

Unless you plan to venture further afield than central Vienna, there's no need to hire a car: the excellent public transport network is a quicker, cheaper and generally more practical way of getting around. However, a car is recommended for discovering off-the-beaten-track parts of the Wienerwald and Wachau Valley. Some trustworthy firms are:

Avis ⓐ Opernring Wien 3 ⓣ 01 587 6241 ⓦ www.avis.com
Europcar ⓐ Schubertring 9 ⓣ 01 714 6717 ⓦ www.europcar.com
Hertz ⓐ Kaerntner Ring 17 ⓣ 01 512 8677 ⓦ www.hertz.co.uk

The impressive Parliament building can be seen from the Ring

THE CITY OF

Vienna

The city centre

Vienna's 1st district, a UNESCO World Heritage Site, is filled with majestic Habsburg palaces and chandelier-lit coffee houses, some of the world's finest galleries and hip bars lining the Bermuda Triangle. First-timers to the Austrian capital often kick off their stay in the vibrant and walkable centre, with plenty to keep culture buffs, shopaholics and clubbers on their toes for days. Whether you are clip-clopping through the Innere Stadt (city centre) in a horse-drawn *Fiaker*, watching puppeteers perform in the shadow of St Stephen's Cathedral or whiling away an afternoon over coffee and cake – this is the Vienna of a thousand postcards.

SIGHTS & ATTRACTIONS

Hofburg (Imperial Palace)

For 600 years the epicentre of the Habsburg Empire, this immense palace complex is overwhelming. You could literally spend days roaming the lavish Imperial Apartments once inhabited by Emperor Franz Josef I and Empress Elisabeth and still festooned with Bohemian crystal chandeliers and Biedermeier portraits. Other highlights include the Sisi Museum, Silver Collection and Imperial Court Chapel where the celebrated Vienna Boys' Choir sings every Sunday. ⓐ Kaisertor/Innerer Burghof ⓣ 01 533 75 70 ⓦ www.hofburg-wien.at ⓛ 09.00–17.30 (Sept–June); 09.00–18.00 (July & Aug) ⓝ U-Bahn: U3 Herrengasse ⓘ Admission charge

Rathaus (Vienna City Hall)

Rising high above the square, Vienna's neo-Gothic City Hall strikes you with its slender 98-m (322-ft) tower and *Eiserner Rathausmann* (Iron Knight). It looks impressive lit up by night. Rathausplatz 01 525 50 Guided tours: 13.00 Mon, Wed & Fri U-Bahn: U2 Rathaus

Ringstrasse (The Ring)

Vienna's city centre is encircled by the Ringstrasse, a boulevard built on the old city walls that's often simply called the Ring.

Hofburg Imperial Palace

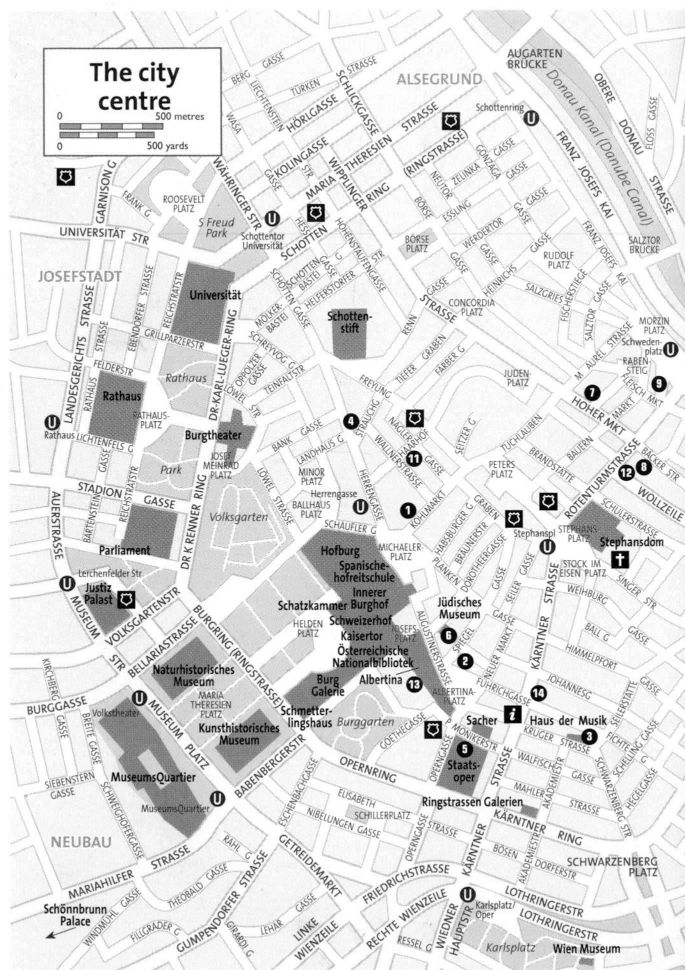
The city centre
0 500 metres
0 500 yards
ALSERGRUND
JOSEFSTADT
NEUBAU
Universität
Rathaus
Burgtheater
Parliament
Justiz Palast
Naturhistorisches Museum
Kunsthistorisches Museum
MuseumsQuartier
Hofburg
Spanische-hofreitschule
Innerer Burghof
Schatzkammer
Schweizerhof
Kaisertor
Österreichische Nationalbibliotek
Albertina
Burg Galerie
Schmetterlingshaus
Burggarten
Volksgarten
Schottenstift
Jüdisches Museum
Sacher
Haus der Musik
Staatsoper
Ringstrassen Galerien
Stephansdom
Karlsplatz
Wien Museum
Schönnbrunn Palace
Donau Kanal (Danube Canal)
Schottenring
Schottentor Universität
Rathaus
Herrengasse
Stephanspl
Volkstheater
MuseumsQuartier
Karlsplatz/ Oper
Schweden-platz
Lerchenfelder Str
S Freud Park
Park
UNIVERSITÄT STR
RINGSTRASSE
OPERNRING
KÄRNTNER RING
KÄRNTNER STRASSE
ROTENTURMSTRASSE
WOLLZEILE
MARIAHILFER STRASSE
FRIEDRICHSTRASSE
LINKE WIENZEILE
RECHTE WIENZEILE
GUMPENDORFER STRASSE
SCHWARZENBERG PLATZ

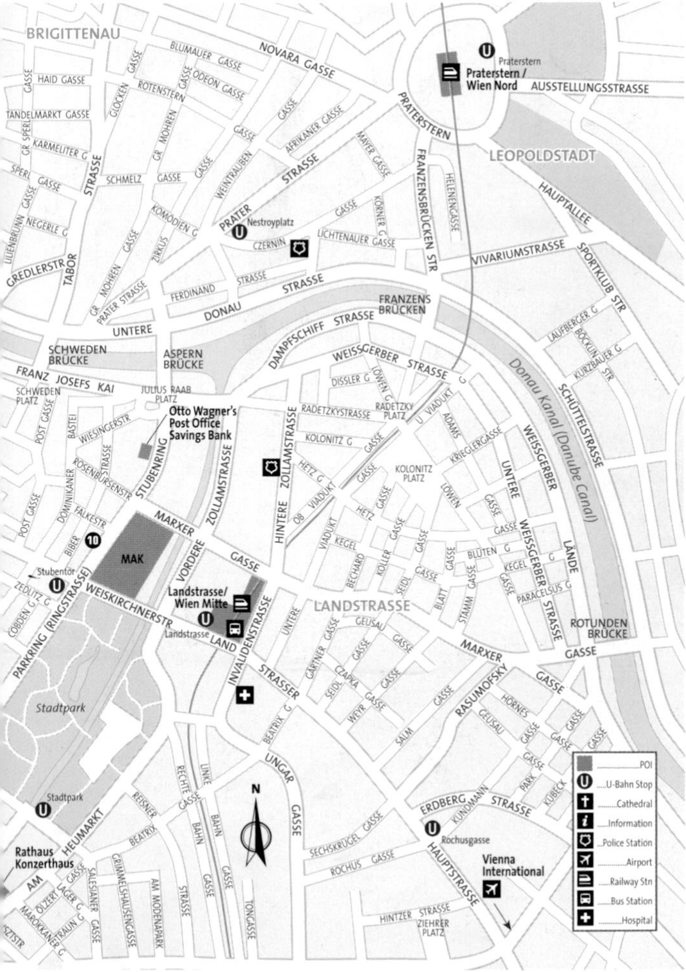
BRIGITTENAU
LEOPOLDSTADT
LANDSTRASSE
Praterstern
Praterstern / Wien Nord
Nestroyplatz
Otto Wagner's Post Office Savings Bank
MAK
Stubentor
Landstrasse/ Wien Mitte
Landstrasse
Stadtpark
Rathaus Konzerthaus
Rochusgasse
Vienna International
Donau Kanal (Danube Canal)
SCHWEDEN BRÜCKE
ASPERN BRÜCKE
FRANZENS BRÜCKEN
ROTUNDEN BRÜCKE
FRANZ JOSEFS KAI
NOVARA GASSE
AUSSTELLUNGSSTRASSE
PRATERSTERN
PRATER STRASSE
HAUPTALLEE
VIVARIUMSTRASSE
UNTERE DONAU STRASSE
DAMPFSCHIFF STRASSE
WEISSGERBER STRASSE
RADETZKYSTRASSE
ZOLLAMSTRASSE
HINTERE ZOLLAMSTRASSE
STUBENRING
MARXER GASSE
WEISKIRCHNERSTR
PARKRING (RINGSTRASSE)
LANDSTRASSER HAUPTSTRASSE
INVALIDENSTRASSE
RASUMOFSKY GASSE
ERDBERG STRASSE
UNGAR GASSE
HEUMARKT
N
POI
U-Bahn Stop
Cathedral
Information
Police Station
Airport
Railway Stn
Bus Station
Hospital

Hop on tram 1 or 2 to see the main sights, which include the Hofburg, the University of Vienna and Otto Wagner's Post Office Savings Bank. ⓦ www.wien.info

Spanische Hofreitschule (Spanish Riding School)
See the Lipizzaner stallions in action at the Hofburg's school for classical riding. Enjoy the morning exercises to music or one of the full performances. ⓐ Michaelerplatz 1 ⓣ 01 533 90 31 ⓦ www.srs.at ⓛ Morning exercises: 10.00–12.00 Tues–Fri; performances: 11.00 Sat & Sun; closed Mon ⓤ U-Bahn: U3 Herrengasse ⓘ Admission charge

Stephansdom (St Stephen's Cathedral)
Soaring above Stephansplatz, this Gothic cathedral is one of Vienna's most iconic landmarks with its skeletal spires and zigzag mosaic-tiled roof (see photo, page 72). The tower, at 137 m (448 ft), was completed in 1433 and was for many years the tallest building in Europe. Climb its 343 steps for far-reaching views

WINGED BEAUTIES
Set in the beautiful Burggarten, the Art Nouveau Schmetterlingshaus (Butterfly House) is alive with tiny wings. Glance up to see more than 400 butterflies fluttering past tropical foliage. You can even get married here. ⓐ Burggarten ⓣ 01 533 8570
ⓦ www.schmetterlingshaus.at ⓛ 10.00–16.45 Mon–Fri, 10.00–18.15 Sat & Sun (Apr–Oct); 10.00–15.45 (Nov–Mar)
ⓤ U-Bahn: U1 Karlsplatz ⓘ Admission charge

over the rooftops. The cathedral's famous bell, the Pummerin, is used to ring in the New Year across the city. Stephansplatz 3 01 515 52 37 67 www.stephanskirche.at 09.00–11.30, 13.00–16.30 Mon–Sat, 13.00–16.30 Sun U-Bahn: U1 Stephansplatz Admission charge

Volksgarten (People's Park)

Speckled with sculptures and fountains, this central pocket of greenery is a breath of fresh air. Stroll the rose gardens, spot the neoclassical Temple of Theseus and marble monument to Empress Elisabeth, then pause for coffee and cake in the octagonal pavilion. Burgring U-Bahn: U3 Volkstheater

CULTURE

Albertina

This grand Habsburg palace houses a vast collection of prints and drawings. The Graphic Collection displays works by Rembrandt, Rubens, and the 20th-century Warhol and Picasso. Keep an eye out for the star of the gallery – Albrecht Dürer's *Feldhase* (young hare) watercolour. Under the same roof is the Photographic Collection, Architecture Collection and Poster Collection. Albertinaplatz 1 01 534 830 www.albertina.at 10.00–18.00 Thur–Tues, 10.00–21.00 Wed U-Bahn: U1 Karlsplatz Admission charge

Burgtheater (National Theatre)

Opened in 1888, this former imperial court theatre stages world-class opera and contemporary and classic plays. The repertoire

and opulent interior are impressive. ⓐ Dr-Karl-Lueger-Ring 2 ⓣ 01 514 44/41 40 ⓦ www.burgtheater.at ◷ Sept–June (performance hours vary) ⓤ U-Bahn: U2 Rathaus

Haus der Musik (House of Music)

Get loud at this state-of-the-art museum with larger-than-life instruments. Compose your own waltz with the Waltz Dice game, create a CD in the Evolution Machine or conduct the Vienna Philharmonic (virtually, of course!). ⓐ Seilerstätte 30 ⓣ 01 513 48 50 ⓦ www.hausdermusik.com ◷ 10.00–22.00 daily ⓤ U-Bahn: U1 Karlsplatz ⓘ Admission charge

Jüdisches Museum (Jewish Museum)

Set in a historic mansion, this thought-provoking museum has a permanent exhibition on medieval Jewry and showcases the excavations of a medieval synagogue. ⓐ Dorotheergasse 11 & Judenplatz 8 ⓣ 01 535 04 31 ⓦ www.jmw.at ◷ 10.00–18.00 Sun–Fri, closed Sat ⓤ U-Bahn: U1 Stephansplatz ⓘ Admission charge

Kunsthistorisches Museum (Art History Museum)

Feast your eyes on yet more of the House of Habsburg's art treasures. The domed Renaissance-style museum houses a wonderful collection. The walls of the Picture Gallery are hung with works by Rubens, Caravaggio and Titian, and there are supplementary collections including Egyptian antiquities and Roman pottery. ⓐ Maria-Theresien-Platz ⓣ 01 525 240 ⓦ www.khm.at ◷ 10.00–18.00 Tues, Wed, Fri–Sun, 10.00–21.00 Thur, closed Mon ⓤ U-Bahn: U3 Volkstheater ⓘ Admission charge

The Mozart statue in the Burggarten

MAK (Museum of Applied Arts)

MAK's rich collection stretches from *Wiener Werkstätte* pieces, Art Deco friezes, medieval silk embroideries and Persian carpets right up to architectural models by Frank Gehry. ⓐ Stubenring 5 ⓣ 01 711 360 ⓦ www.mak.at ⓛ 10.00–24.00 Tues, 10.00–18.00 Wed–Sun, closed Mon ⓝ U-Bahn: U3 Stubentor ⓘ Admission charge

Österreichische Nationalbibliothek (Austrian National Library)

Gaze up at the State Hall's frescoes in Europe's largest Baroque library, which houses a Globe Museum and Papyrus Museum tracing life in Ancient Egypt, a collection of writings by Martin Luther and thousands of priceless books. ⓐ Josefsplatz 1 ⓣ 01 534 10 ⓦ www.onb.ac.at ⓛ 10.00–18.00 Sat–Wed, 10.00–21.00 Thur, closed Fri ⓝ U-Bahn: U1 Stephansplatz ⓘ Admission charge

Schatzkammer (Imperial Treasury)

Glittering with jewel-encrusted orbs, vestments and crowns, the wealth of the Hofburg treasury is truly mind-boggling. Take a peek at the Holy Roman Empire jewels. ⓐ Schweizerhof ⓣ 01 525 240 ⓦ www.khm.at ⓛ 10.00–18.00 Wed–Mon, closed Tues ⓝ U-Bahn: U1 Stephansplatz ⓘ Admission charge

Staatsoper (Vienna State Opera)

Vienna's 19th-century opera house is one of the world's greatest. As well as performances by the acclaimed Philharmonic Orchestra, the venue stages first-rate opera and ballet and special performances for children. ⓐ Opernring 2 ⓣ 01 513 15 13 ⓦ www.wiener-staatsoper.at ⓝ U-Bahn: U1 Karlsplatz

RETAIL THERAPY

Altmann & Kühne Marzipan, candied violets and famous *Liliputkonfekt* (miniature chocolates) are lovingly hand wrapped at this old-fashioned sweet store. Am Graben 30 01 533 09 27 www.feinspitz.com 09.00–18.30 Mon–Fri, 10.00–17.00 Sat, closed Sun U-Bahn: U1 Stephansplatz

Augarten Highly coveted by collectors, Augarten porcelain is for sale (at a price) at this flagship store just off Stephansplatz. Look out for classic designs such as the Vienna Rose and Maria Theresia. Stock-im-Eisen-Platz 3 01 512 14 94 www. augarten.at 10.00–18.00 Mon–Sat, closed Sun U-Bahn: U1 Stephansplatz

Boehle Hundreds of Austrian and international wines share shelf space with pâtés and preserves. Wollzeile 30 01 512 31 55 www.boehle.at 08.30–19.00 Mon–Fri, 08.30–17.00 Sat, closed Sun U-Bahn: U3 Stubentor

Meinl am Graben Foodies sniff out specialities like Wachau apricot jam, Mozartkugeln pralines and Spanish *pata negra* ham here. Am Graben 19 01 532 33 34 www.meinlamgraben.at 08.00–19.30 Mon–Fri, 09.00–18.00 Sat, closed Sun U-Bahn: U1 Stephansplatz

Österreichische Werkstätten Quality Austrian handicrafts from glassware to jewellery fill this store. Kärntner Str. 6 01 512 24 18 www.austrianarts.at 10.00–18.30 Mon–Fri, 10.00–18.00 Sat, closed Sun U-Bahn: U1 Stephansplatz

Ringstrassen Galerien This smart shopping centre is the place to buy Aigner shoes and Swarovski crystals. There's also a florist, perfumery, juice joint and a splendid sushi bar if you need to refuel between bouts of retail therapy. ⓐ Kärntner Ring 5–7 ⓣ 01 512 51 81 ⓦ www.ringstrassen-galerien.at ⓛ 10.00–19.00 Mon–Fri, 10.00–18.00 Sat, closed Sun ⓤ U-Bahn: U1 Karlsplatz

Steffl From MAC cosmetics to designer gear by Armani and Esprit, this sleek department store houses 50 shops under one roof. ⓐ Kärntner Str. 19 ⓣ 01 514 310 ⓦ www.kaufhaus-steffl.at ⓛ 09.30–19.00 Mon–Wed, 09.30–20.00 Thur & Fri, 09.30–18.00 Sat, closed Sun ⓤ U-Bahn: U1 Stephansplatz

Swarovski Crystal Store Sauntering along Kärntnerstrasse, you can't miss Swarovski's flagship store, sparkling with jewellery, accessories and collectibles. ⓐ Kärntnerstrasse 8 ⓣ 01 512 90 32 33 ⓦ www.swarovski.com ⓛ 10.00–19.00 Mon–Fri, 10.00–18.00 Sat, closed Sun ⓤ U-Bahn: U1 Stephansplatz

TAKING A BREAK

Café Demel £ ❶ Indulge in pastries or dainty sandwiches with coffee in the beautifully preserved rococo salon and pick up a bag of the famous candied violets before you leave. ⓐ Kohlmarkt 14 ⓣ 01 535 17 170 ⓦ www.demel.at ⓛ 09.00–19.00 daily ⓤ U-Bahn: U3 Herrengasse

Café Tirolerhof £ ❷ Opposite the Albertina, this traditional Viennese coffee house whips up strong coffee and a mean apple strudel. ⓐ Führichgasse 8 ⓣ 01 512 78 33 ⓛ 07.00–22.00 Mon–Sat, 08.30–20.00 Sun ⓝ U-Bahn: U1 Karlsplatz

Cantino £ ❸ On the top floor of the House of Music, this restaurant overlooking St Stephen's offers value-for-money lunches such as ricotta ravioli and pumpkin risotto. ⓐ Seilerstätte 30 ⓣ 01 512 54 46 ⓦ www.cantino.at ⓛ 12.00–15.00, 18.00–23.00 Mon–Fri, 18.00–23.00 Sat, 12.00–15.00 Sun ⓝ U-Bahn: U1 Karlsplatz

Central £ ❹ Vaulted ceilings, marble columns and daily piano music (17.00–22.00) add a dash of old-world grandeur to this literary coffee house. Bow-tied waiters bustle to and fro with decadent cakes and Austrian dishes. ⓐ Herrengasse/Strauchgasse ⓣ 01 533 37 64 26 ⓦ www.palaisevents.at ⓛ 07.30–22.00 Mon–Sat, 10.00–22.00 Sun ⓝ U-Bahn: U3 Herrengasse

Sacher £ ❺ If you want to try the mother of all *Sachertorte* chocolate cakes (baked according to the original 1832 recipe), head for this sublime chandelier-lit Viennese café. ⓐ Philharmonikerstr. 4 ⓣ 01 514 560 ⓦ www.sacher.com ⓛ 08.00–24.00 daily ⓝ U-Bahn: U1 Karlsplatz

Trzesniewski £ ❻ Little gem of a café, with some of Vienna's best open sandwiches. Try them with a *Pfiff* – the tiniest beer you've ever seen. ⓐ Dorotheergasse 1 ⓣ 01 512 32 91 ⓦ www.trzesniewski.at ⓛ 08.30–19.30 Mon–Fri, 09.00–17.00 Sat, closed Sun ⓝ U-Bahn: U1 Stephansplatz

Würstelstand am Hohen Markt £ ❼ The Viennese will tell you that there are simply no better sausages than the ones at this humble stand – and they're absolutely right. For a couple of euros you can treat yourself to a cheese-loaded *Käsekrainer* or *Bratwurst*, served with bread and mustard. ⓐ Hoher Markt 1010 ⏲ 07.00–04.00 daily Ⓝ Bus: 1A, 2A Hoher Markt

Zanoni & Zanoni £ ❽ Refresh with *gelati*, a prosciutto *panini* or espresso on the terrace of this excellent Italian ice-cream parlour. ⓐ Lugeck 7, off Rotenturmstr. ⓣ 01 512 79 79 ⓦ www.zanoni.co.at ⏲ 07.00–24.00 daily Ⓝ U-Bahn: U1 Stephansplatz

AFTER DARK

RESTAURANTS

Bermuda Bräu £ ❾ Tuck into Austrian favourites like *schnitzel* and goulash, washed down with homebrews, in this lively gastro-pub. ⓐ Rabensteig 6 ⓣ 01 532 28 65 ⓦ www.bermuda-braeu.at ⏲ 11.00–04.00 Mon–Sat, 11.00–02.00 Sun Ⓝ U-Bahn: U1 Schwedenplatz

Comida £ ❿ Spice up your evening with Caribbean specialities like jerk chicken, goat curry and chilli-fuelled 'pepper pot' made to make your eyes water. Sip mojitos or daiquiris at the rum bar. ⓐ Stubenring 20 ⓣ 01 512 40 24 ⓦ www.comida.at ⏲ 11.00–01.00 Mon–Fri, 18.00–01.00 Sat & Sun Ⓝ U-Bahn: U3 Stubentor

Esterházykeller £ ⓫ Go underground to this vaulted 17th-century *Heurige* (wine cellar) with exposed brickwork, wood panelling and an impressive wine list. Hearty fare includes pork roast, dumplings and strudel. ⓐ Haarhof 1 ⓣ 01 533 34 82 ⓦ www.esterhazykeller.at ⓛ 11.00–23.00 daily ⓝ U-Bahn: U3 Herrengasse

Figlmuller ££ ⓬ Golden, crisp and absolutely huge – the Wiener Schnitzel at this brick-vaulted tavern in the heart of the Innere stadt are legendary. Bring an appetite. ⓐ Wollzeile 5 ⓣ 01 512 61 77 ⓦ www.figlmueller.at ⓛ 11.00–22.30 daily ⓝ U-Bahn: U3 Stephansplatz

Palmenhaus ££ ⓭ Dine beneath palms and vines at the Art Nouveau Palmenhaus, a glorious glass-fronted conservatory with views over the Burggarten and Hofburg palace. ⓐ Burggarten ⓣ 01 533 10 33 ⓦ www.palmenhaus.at ⓛ 10.00–02.00 (Mar–Oct); 11.30–24.00 (Nov–Feb) ⓝ U-Bahn: U1 Karlsplatz

Sky Bar £££ ⓮ Going up... spy St Stephen's Cathedral from the seventh-floor Sky Bar. All floor-to-ceiling glass, this place isn't cheap, but the cuisine is gourmet and views are priceless. ⓐ Kärntner Str. 19 ⓣ 01 513 17 12 ⓦ www.skybar.at ⓛ 13.00–03.00 Mon–Sat, 18.00–02.00 Sun ⓝ U-Bahn: U1 Stephansplatz

BARS & CLUBS

Club Habana Get your Latino groove on and sway all night long to salsa, bachata and merengue. ⓐ Mahlerstr. 11 ⓣ 01 513 20 75

The Do & Co Hotel has great views of St Stephen's Cathedral

www.clubhabana.at 22.00–06.00 Fri & Sat U-Bahn: U1 Karlsplatz

Flex Bass-loaded club beside the Danube Canal with live acts and DJs spinning techno, electro and drum 'n' bass beats. Donaukanal 1 01 533 75 25 www.flex.at 20.00–04.00 daily U-Bahn: U2 Schottenring

Jazzland This cellar bar has been jazzing up Vienna's after-dark scene since 1972, with live music from 21.00 six times a week. Franz Josefs Kai 29 01 533 25 75 www.jazzland.at 19.00–late Mon–Sat, closed Sun U-Bahn: U1 Schwedenplatz

Krah Krah Laid-back pub serving 50 different kinds of beer. Rabensteig 8 01 533 81 93 www.krah-krah.at 11.00–02.00 Mon–Sat, 11.00–01.00 Sun U-Bahn: U1 Schwedenplatz

Pavillon & Volksgarten This open-air café and club duo is the best spot to see the Imperial Palace twinkle after dark. Sip a cocktail under the chestnut trees or join a good-looking crowd on the dance floor at the weekend. Burgring 01 532 42 41 www.volksgarten.at Pavillon: 11.00–02.00 daily; Volksgarten: 23.00–06.00 Fri & Sat U-Bahn: U2 Volkstheater

Red Room This is one of Vienna's most glamorous lounge bars, wth backlit ceilings and vampy scarlet walls. DJs playing R'n'B and soul keep the dance floor full. Stubenring 20 01 512 40 24 www.comida.at 20.00–late Mon–Sat, closed Sun U-Bahn: U3 Stubentor

Neubau & Mariahilf

So you've done your Habsburg palace bit, now head over to the 7th district to see what they've done to the imperial stables. They've turned into the dynamic MuseumsQuartier – one of the ten biggest cultural complexes in the world – harbouring galleries, event spaces, restaurants, cafés and boutiques. Dance, contemporary art, the latest in Viennese fashion – this is Vienna's hotspot for cutting-edge culture and design.

SIGHTS & ATTRACTIONS

quartier21

A vast space given over to independent cultural initiatives, contemporary arts and idiosyncratic shops, and with a thriving artist-in-residence scheme, quartier21 has plenty of surprises tucked up its sleeve. Rock down to Electric Avenue's galleries and boutiques, or discover the illuminated Tonspur passage, Play FM and Puls TV, Vienna's first local TV station.
ⓐ Museumsplatz 1 ⓦ http://quartier21.mqw.at
U-Bahn: U2 MuseumsQuartier

Spittelberg

Explore the Spittelberg's maze of narrow cobbled streets for a taste of old Vienna with a modern twist. Having been given a new lease of life, this has become one of the city's hippest enclaves, with a string of grand 19th-century Biedermeier houses, open-air cafés, hole-in-the-wall pubs, dinky art galleries and vibrant bars. ⓦ www.spittelberg.at U-Bahn: U3 Volkstheater

Visit art galleries and studios in quartier21

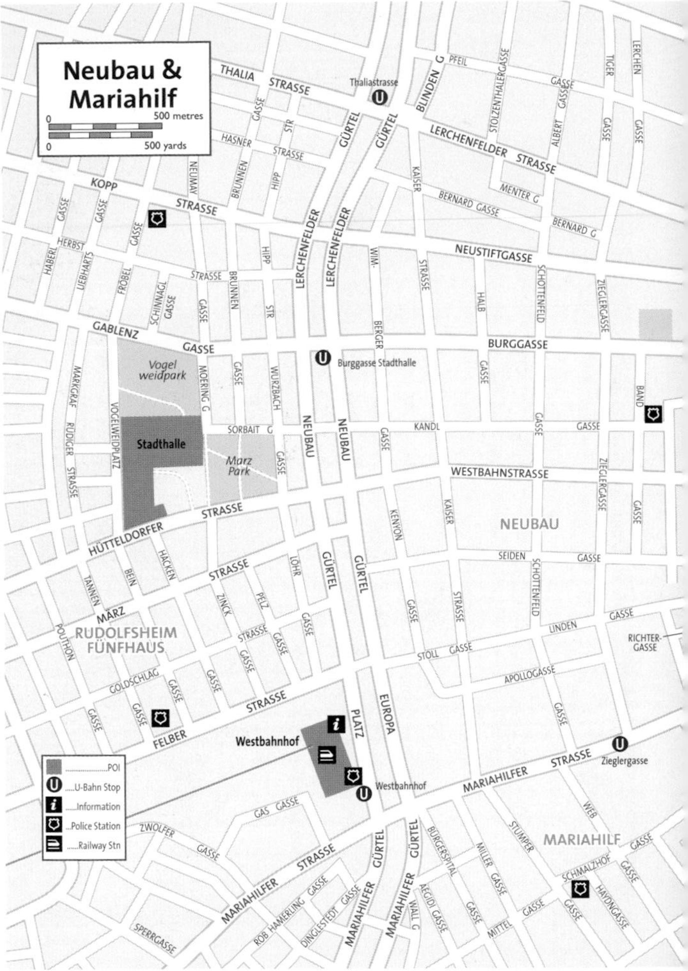
Neubau &
Mariahilf
0
500 metres
0
500 yards
POI
U-Bahn Stop
Information
Police Station
Railway Stn
Thaliastrasse
Burggasse Stadthalle
Westbahnhof
Zieglergasse
Vogel weidpark
Stadthalle
Marz Park
Westbahnhof
NEUBAU
RUDOLFSHEIM FÜNFHAUS
MARIAHILF
THALIA STRASSE
LERCHENFELDER STRASSE
NEUSTIFTGASSE
BURGGASSE
WESTBAHNSTRASSE
KANDL GASSE
SEIDEN GASSE
LINDEN GASSE
STOLL GASSE
APOLLOGASSE
MARIAHILFER STRASSE
GABLENZ GASSE
HÜTTELDORFER STRASSE
MÄRZ STRASSE
FELBER STRASSE
KOPP STRASSE
GÜRTEL
NEUBAU GÜRTEL
LERCHENFELDER GÜRTEL
EUROPA PLATZ
SORBAIT G
MOERING G
VOGELWEIDPLATZ
RÜDIGER STRASSE
MARKGRAF
ZIEGLERGASSE
SCHOTTENFELD GASSE
KAISER STRASSE
KENYON GASSE
BERNARD GASSE
BERNARD G
MENTER G
STOLZENTHALERGASSE
ALBERT GASSE
BLINDEN G
PFEIL GASSE
TIGER GASSE
LERCHEN GASSE
HASNER STRASSE
NEUMAY GASSE
BRUNNEN GASSE
HIPP STR
WIM- BERGER
HALB GASSE
BAND GASSE
RICHTER- GASSE
SCHMALZHOF GASSE
HAYDNGASSE
STUMPER GASSE
MILLER GASSE
MITTEL GASSE
WEB GASSE
BÜRGERSPITAL GASSE
AEGIDI GASSE
WALL G
MARIAHILFER GÜRTEL
DINGLESTEDT GASSE
ROB HAMERLING GASSE
GAS GASSE
ZWÖLFER GASSE
SPERRGASSE
GOLDSCHLAG STRASSE
POUTHON GASSE
TANNEN GASSE
BEIN GASSE
HACKEN GASSE
ZINCK GASSE
PELZ GASSE
LÖHR GASSE
WURZBACH GASSE
SCHINNAGL GASSE
FRÖBEL GASSE
LIEBHARTS GASSE
HABERL GASSE
HERBST STRASSE

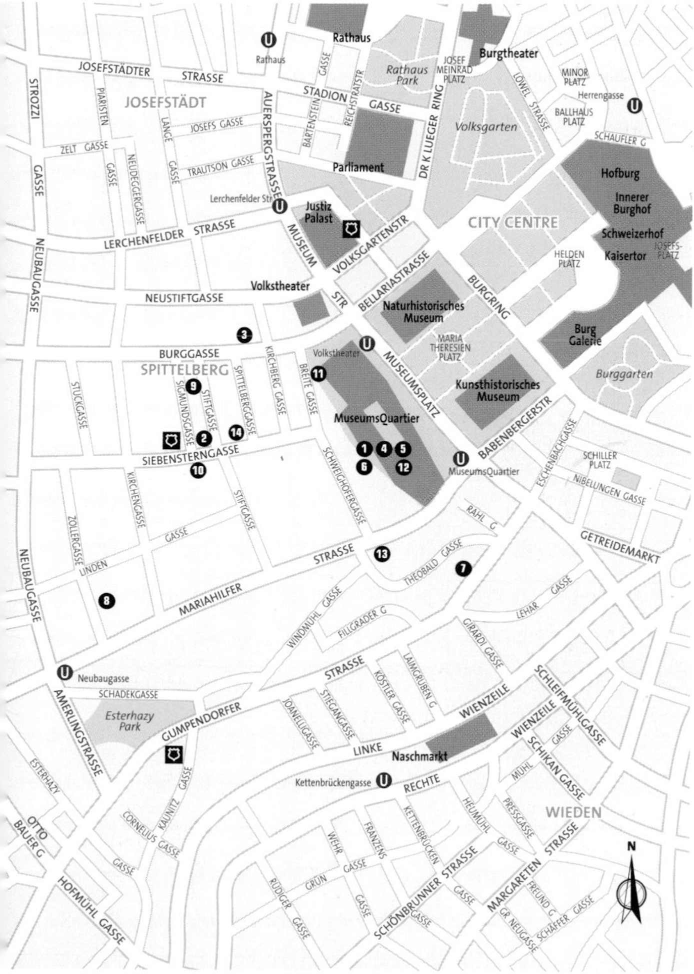

Rathaus
Rathaus Park
JOSEF MEINRAD PLATZ
Burgtheater
MINOR PLATZ
Herrengasse
BALLHAUS PLATZ
JOSEFSTÄDTER STRASSE
STROZZI GASSE
JOSEFSTÄDT
PIARISTEN GASSE
LANGE GASSE
JOSEFS GASSE
AUERSPERGSTRASSE
STADION GASSE
BARTENSTEIN G
REICHSRATSSTR
DR K LUEGER RING
Volksgarten
LÖWEL STRASSE
SCHAUFLER G
ZELT GASSE
NEUDEGGERGASSE
TRAUTSON GASSE
Parliament
Hofburg
Innerer Burghof
Schweizerhof
Kaiserto
JOSEFS-PLATZ
Lerchenfelder Str
Justiz Palast
LERCHENFELDER STRASSE
MUSEUM STR
VOLKSGARTENSTR
CITY CENTRE
HELDEN PLATZ
NEUBAUGASSE
BELLARIASTRASSE
Volkstheater
NEUSTIFTGASSE
Naturhistorisches Museum
BURGRING
Burg Galerie
Burggarten
BURGGASSE
SPITTELBERG
Volkstheater
MARIA THERESIEN PLATZ
MUSEUMSPLATZ
Kunsthistorisches Museum
STUCKGASSE
SIGMUNDSGASSE
STIFTGASSE
SPITTELBERGGASSE
KIRCHBERG GASSE
BREITE GASSE
MuseumsQuartier
BABENBERGERSTR
ESCHENBACHGASSE
SCHILLER PLATZ
NIBELUNGEN GASSE
SIEBENSTERNGASSE
SCHWEIGHOFERGASSE
MuseumsQuartier
KIRCHENGASSE
STIFTGASSE
RAHL G
ZOLLERGASSE
LINDEN GASSE
GETREIDEMARKT
MARIAHILFER STRASSE
THEOBALD GASSE
LEHAR GASSE
WINDMÜHL GASSE
FILLGRADER G
GIRARDI GASSE
Neubaugasse
SCHADEKGASSE
LAIMGRUBEN G
KÖSTLER GASSE
STIEGANGASSE
JOANELLIGASSE
GUMPENDORFER STRASSE
Esterhazy Park
AMERLINGSTRASSE
WIENZEILE
SCHLEIFMÜHLGASSE
LINKE WIENZEILE
Naschmarkt
MÜHL GASSE
SCHIKAN GASSE
ESTERHAZY
Kettenbrückengasse
RECHTE WIENZEILE
WIEDEN
KAUNITZ GASSE
CORNELIUS GASSE
OTTO BAUER G
HEUMÜHL GASSE
PRESSGASSE
KETTENBRÜCKEN GASSE
FRANZENS GASSE
WEHR GASSE
GRÜN GASSE
RÜDIGER GASSE
SCHÖNBRUNNER STRASSE
MARGARETEN STRASSE
FREUND G
GR NEUGASSE
SCHÄFFER GASSE
HOFMÜHL GASSE
N

CULTURE

Architekturzentrum Wien

White walls, arches and sleek staircases set the scene for changing exhibitions, talks and workshops. Look out for the F3 Hall's vaulting, the octagonal library's skylight and the Old Hall's exposed brickwork. a Museumsplatz 1 t 01 522 31 15 w www.azw.at 10.00–19.00 daily U-Bahn: U2 MuseumsQuartier ! Admission charge

Dschungel Wien

Challenging conventions, this theatre aims its unique productions and workshops at young audiences. Alongside puppetry, dance and theatre, new media and experimental works play a big part. a Museumsplatz 1 t 01 522 07 20 w www.dschungelwien.at Opening hours depend on the event being staged so check website for details U-Bahn: U2 MuseumsQuartier

Halle E & G

Perched on the site of the former court stables and fusing Baroque with modern architecture, this art space is a real audience grabber, hosting pioneering theatre, dance, music and opera, and the annual ImPulsTanz dance festival. a Museumsplatz 1 t 01 524 33 210 w www.halleneg.at 10.00–19.00 Mon–Sat, closed Sun U-Bahn: U2 MuseumsQuartier

Kunsthalle Wien

Enjoy experimental art in its different guises at this innovative museum. The 18th-century cream-coloured edifice has been

MUMOK (MUSEUM OF MODERN ART LUDWIG FOUNDATION)

This grey lava-stone megalith houses Austria's largest contemporary art museum. Its collection spans 7,000 works covering the major 20th-century movements. The big names exhibited include Picasso, Magritte, Kandinsky, Klee and Warhol. ⓐ Museumsplatz 1 ⓣ 01 525 00 ⓦ www.mumok.at ◷ 10.00–18.00 Fri–Wed, 10.00–21.00 Thur ⓡ U-Bahn: U2 MuseumsQuartier ⓘ Admission charge

revamped as a multimedia forum for contemporary paintings, photography, film and new media. ⓐ Museumsplatz 1 ⓣ 01 521 89 12 01 ⓦ www.kunsthallewien.at ◷ 10.00–21.00 Thur, 10.00–19.00 Fri–Wed ⓡ U-Bahn: U2 MuseumsQuartier ⓘ Admission charge

Leopold Museum

Set in a vast white limestone cube, the museum houses Rudolf Leopold's formerly private collection. The light-flooded galleries showcase 19th- and 20th-century masterpieces on five levels, including important works by Gustav Klimt, Oskar Kokoschka, Egon Schiele and Herbert Boeckl. Klimt's mosaic-like *Tod und Leben* (Death and Life) raises eyebrows. ⓐ Museumsplatz 1 ⓣ 01 525 700 ⓦ www.leopoldmuseum.org ◷ 10.00–18.00 Fri–Wed, 10.00–21.00 Thur ⓡ U-Bahn: U2 MuseumsQuartier ⓘ Admission charge

Tanzquartier Wien

Cutting-edge centre for contemporary choreographies, bringing the best of national and international dance to the MuseumsQuartier. ⓐ Museumsplatz 1 ⓣ 01 581 35 91 ⓦ www.tqw.at Opening hours depend on the event being staged so check website for details U-Bahn: U2 MuseumsQuartier

Volkstheater (People's Theatre)

This *fin-de-siècle* theatre shows an eclectic mix of classics, new plays and avant-garde interpretations from Shakespeare to *chanson*. Sip drinks beneath the chandeliers in the frescoed Rote Bar before the performance. ⓐ Neustiftgasse 1 ⓣ 01 521 110 ⓦ www.volkstheater.at Opening hours depend on the event

Old meets new in MuseumsQuartier

- **Staatsoper (Vienna State Opera)** See world-class opera and ballet at the 19th-century Opera House (see page 66).
- **Österreichische Galerie Belvedere (Belvedere Gallery)** Roam manicured gardens and see Klimt's *The Kiss* (1908) at Prince Eugene of Savoy's rococo summer palace (see page 95).
- **Hundertwasserhaus** Curvy walls, shimmering mosaics and a rainbow of colours characterise Friedensreich Hundertwasser's house (see page 89).
- **Sacher** Indulge in rich *Sachertorte* chocolate cake filled with tangy apricot jam and baked according to a secret recipe at this decadent Viennese coffee house (see page 69).
- **Kunsthistorisches Museum** Filled with Habsburg treasures including Old Master paintings by the likes of Rubens and Titian (see page 64).
- **Spittelberg** Old Vienna meets new in this hip district interlaced with narrow streets and dotted with Biedermeier houses, open-air cafés and kooky galleries (see page 74).

The Kunsthistorisches Museum

being staged so check website for details U-Bahn: U3 Volkstheater

ZOOM Kindermuseum

Kids can pull and prod in the Zoom Ozean, or create cartoons and record their own music in the Zoom Lab at Austria's only children's museum. Activities need to be pre-booked. Museumsplatz 1 01 524 79 08 www.kindermuseum.at 08.30–16.00 daily U-Bahn: U2 MuseumsQuartier Admission charge

RETAIL THERAPY

Be a Good Girl Divas with attitude pick up quirky shoes, shirts and bags, slip into a new pair of Levi's and get their hair snipped in the salon. Westbahnstr. 5A 01 524 47 28 www.beagoodgirl.com 10.00–19.00 Tues–Fri, 10.00–16.00 Sat, closed Sun & Mon Bus 13A: Zieglergasse

Buchhandlung Walther König Browse for books on art, photography, design and architecture in this vaulted Baroque hall, which doubles as a platform for lectures, presentations and literary events. Museumsplatz 1 01 512 85 88 www.buchhandlung-walther-koenig.de 10.00–19.00 Mon–Sat, 12.00–19.00 Sun U-Bahn: U2 MuseumsQuartier

Filz Faktor Trendy textile store where everything is made from felt, ranging from brightly coloured berets and bags

to soft slippers and scarves. ⓐ Neubaugasse 11 ⓣ 01 944 66 55 ⓦ www.filzfaktor.at ◷ 10.00–18.00 Mon–Wed & Fri, 10.00–19.00 Thur, 10.00–17.00 Sat, closed Sun ⓝ U-Bahn: U3 Volkstheater

Milk & Honey Psychedelic boutique with colourful clothing and original gifts from holograms and acid jazz records to wacky lamps and spray-painted toasters. ⓐ Zollergasse 16 ⓣ 01 923 93 99 ⓦ www.milkandhoney.at ◷ 11.00–19.00 Mon–Fri, 10.00–19.00 Sat, closed Sun ⓝ U-Bahn: U3 Neubaugasse

Peek & Cloppenburg Fashionistas flock to this department store giant, which stocks labels like Adidas, Armani, Betty Barclay, Burberry, Diesel and Miss Sixty. ⓐ Mariahilfer Str. 26–30 ⓣ 01 525 610 ⓦ www.peekundcloppenburg.at ◷ 10.00–19.00 Mon–Wed, 10.00–20.00 Thur & Fri, 09.30–18.00 Sat, closed Sun ⓝ U-Bahn: U3 Neubaugasse

Styleaut Styleaut is the must-shop boutique for home-grown Austrian fashion and accessories. The store is a platform for emerging and established designers, with styles ranging from 'feminine chic' to urban street wear. ⓐ Museumsplatz 1 ⓦ www.styleaut.com ◷ 13.00–19.00 Tues–Sat, closed Sun & Mon ⓝ U-Bahn: U2 MuseumsQuartier

Subotron Game freaks seek out technical wizardry at this electronics store. Test out the latest PC games, gadgets and music before you buy. ⓐ Museumsplatz 1 ⓦ www.subotron.com ◷ 13.00–18.00 Wed–Sun, closed Mon & Tues ⓝ U-Bahn: U2 MuseumsQuartier

TAKING A BREAK

Café Leopold £ ❶ This ultra-modern café's huge windows and terrace afford prime views over the MuseumsQuartier. By night, it becomes a hip bar with DJs on the decks and film screenings. ⓐ Museumsplatz 1 ⓣ 01 523 67 32 ⓦ www.cafe-leopold.at ⏲ 10.00–02.00 Sun–Wed, 10.00–04.00 Thur–Sat ⓣ U-Bahn: U2 MuseumsQuartier

Centimeter £ ❷ Order sandwiches by the centimetre and beer by the litre at this fun spot. ⓐ Stiftgasse 4 ⓣ 01 470 06 06 ⓦ www.centimeter.at ⏲ 11.00–24.00 Mon–Thur, 11.00–01.00 Fri & Sat, closed Sun ⓣ U-Bahn: U3 Volkstheater

Das Möbel is a stylish café and gallery in one

Das Möbel £ ❸ A lunch spot and interior design gallery rolled into one. You can buy the chair you sit on if you've got the cash. The airy café serves snacks like fresh salads, quiches, sandwiches and pastries. Try the ginger-lemon tea with banana cake. ⓐ Burggasse 10 ⓣ 01 524 94 97 ⓦ www.dasmoebel.at ◷ 10.00–01.00 daily Ⓝ U-Bahn: U3 Volkstheater

Milo £ ❹ Striking café with a vaulted, black-and-white tiled ceiling. The oriental-inspired artwork makes this a great spot to take a break and check out the moreish menu. ⓐ Museumsplatz 1 ⓣ 01 523 65 66 ◷ 12.00–24.00 Mon–Fri, 10.00–24.00 Sat, 10.00–18.00 Sun Ⓝ U-Bahn: U2 MuseumsQuartier

MQdaily £ ❺ Pause for organic coffee and snacks to eat in or take away at this health-inspired shop near the main entrance. ⓐ Museumsplatz 1 ⓣ 01 522 45 24 ⓦ www.mqdaily.at ◷ 09.00–01.00 Mon–Sat, 09.00–24.00 Sun Ⓝ U-Bahn: U2 MuseumsQuartier

MUMOK Café £ ❻ An arched ceiling, glass walls and communal tables create a feeling of space at the MUMOK gallery's open-plan café. The value-for-money lunch menu features Mediterranean-inspired dishes and kids' favourites. It's the perfect place to relax with coffee by day and enjoy cocktails by night. ⓐ Museumsplatz 1 ⓣ 01 525 00 14 40 ⓦ www.mumok.at ◷ 10.00–18.00 Mon–Wed & Fri–Sun, 10.00–21.00 Thur, until 24.00 when the weather is fine Ⓝ U-Bahn: U2 MuseumsQuartier

Sperl Concert Café £ ❼ With its dark wood panelling and low lighting, this Art Nouveau haunt is (justifiably) one of Vienna's most popular coffee houses. Sip a double mocha with a slice of chocolatey *Sperltorte* or poppy strudel and read the selection of international newspapers. There's live music on a Sunday afternoon. ⓐ Gumpendorfer Str. 11 ⓣ 01 586 41 58 ⓦ www.cafesperl.at ◷ 07.00–23.00 Mon–Sat, 11.00–20.00 Sun; closed Sun (July & Aug) ⓝ U-Bahn: U2 MuseumsQuartier

St. Art £ ❽ Enjoy a chai latte with ginger and cardamom or freshly pressed juices at this café-cum-gallery. The menu stretches from tasty snacks to exhibitions and live music. ⓐ Zollergasse 6 ⓣ 0680 206 7171 ⓦ www.st-art.at ◷ 16.00–02.00 Mon–Sat, 11.00–20.00 Sun ⓝ U-Bahn: U3 Neubaugasse

AFTER DARK

RESTAURANTS

Amerlingbeisl £ ❾ Munch on tender lamb or tofu with apple chutney beneath a canopy of trees in this relaxed restaurant's inner courtyard. ⓐ Stiftgasse 8 ⓣ 01 526 16 60 ⓦ www.amerlingbeisl.at ◷ 09.00–02.00 Mon–Sat, closed Sun ⓝ U-Bahn: U3 Volkstheater

Epos £ ❿ The design is simple and the food delicious at this Middle Eastern restaurant. Tuck into stuffed vine leaves, lamb and okra stew and sticky baklava. ⓐ Siebensterngasse 13/2 ⓣ 01 526 02 19 ⓦ www.restaurantepos.at ◷ 11.00–23.00 Mon–Sat, closed Sun ⓝ U-Bahn: U3 Volkstheater

Glacis Beisl £ ⓫ Pull up a chair on the tree-fringed terrace or in the conservatory for Viennese fare like organic beef goulash with pickles and home-made pancakes with apricot jam from the Wachau. Quirky touches here include the aquarium and a 'growing picture' – a wall sprouting plants and flowers. ⓐ Breite Gasse 4 ⓣ 01 526 56 60 ⓦ www.glacisbeisl.at ⓛ 11.00–02.00 daily ⓝ U-Bahn: U2 MuseumsQuartier

Halle £ ⓬ Cylindrical lights, arched windows and sheer drapes set the scene at this high-ceilinged restaurant, where you can dine on Italian flavours such as polenta with porcini mushrooms or relax with drinks on the buzzy terrace. ⓐ Museumsplatz 1 ⓣ 01 523 70 01 ⓦ www.motto.at ⓛ 10.00–02.00 daily ⓝ U-Bahn: U2 MuseumsQuartier

Bar Italia ££ ⓭ One of the coolest places to dine in the 7th district, this Italian restaurant serves specialities like wild garlic ravioli and octopus carpaccio with salsa verde. Sip cocktails at the low-lit bar. ⓐ Mariahilfer Str. 19–21 ⓣ 01 585 28 38 ⓦ www.baritalia.net ⓛ 18.30–02.00 Tues–Sat, closed Sun & Mon ⓝ U-Bahn: U3 Neubaugasse

Bohème ££ ⓮ Savour Austrian fusion cuisine at this snug restaurant with a cavernous wine cellar. Seafood lovers can sample dishes like Norwegian salmon and monkfish with a glass of crisp Grüner Veltliner. ⓐ Spittelberggasse 19 ⓣ 01 523 31 73 ⓦ www.boheme.at ⓛ 11.00–24.00 daily ⓝ U-Bahn: U3 Volkstheater

BARS & CLUBS

Blue Box Chilled café where the DJs spin everything from electro and techno beats to soul and ska. ⓐ Richtergasse 8 ⓣ 01 523 26 82 ⓦ www.bluebox.at ◷ 10.00–02.00 Mon–Thur, 10.00–04.00 Fri & Sat, closed Sun ⓤ U-Bahn: U3 Neubaugasse

Kantine Sip cocktails at the onyx bar of this high-ceilinged venue decked out with oversized glitter balls and squishy sofas. ⓐ Museumsplatz 1 ⓣ 01 523 82 39 ◷ 09.00–02.00 Mon–Sat, 09.00–24.00 Sun ⓤ U-Bahn: U2 MuseumsQuartier

Lux Immerse yourself in the buzzing street life of Spittelberg at this sleek lounge bar and café, where a young crowd spills out on to the cobbles in summer. ⓐ Spittelberggasse 3 ⓣ 01 526 94 91 ⓦ www.lux-restaurant.at ◷ 11.00–01.00 Mon–Fri, 10.00–01.00 Sat & Sun ⓤ U-Bahn: U2 MuseumsQuartier

rhiz Vienna DJs and bands play everything from alternative electro to experimental rock at this laid-back bar-cum-club under the railway arches. Expect a friendly crowd and a packed dance floor. ⓐ Lerchenfelder Gürtel/Stadtbahnbogen 37 ⓣ 01 409 2505 ⓦ www.rhiz.org ◷ 18.00–04.00 Mon–Sat, closed Sun ⓤ U-Bahn: U3 Stephansplatz

Siebenstern Bräu Drink homebrews beside copper kegs at this Spittelberg haunt. The adventurous can slurp fiery 7 Stern chilli beer or Bamberger Rauchbier, which is smoked over beechwood. ⓐ Siebensterngasse 19 ⓣ 01 523 86 97 ⓦ www.7stern.at ◷ 10.00–24.00 daily ⓤ U-Bahn: U3 Volkstheater

Leopoldstadt & Landstrasse

With the Prater's big wheel going round and Hundertwasser's crazy colours turning heads, Vienna's 2nd and 3rd districts are bound to put a spring in your step.

Whether you want to drift along the Danube to drink in the city's sights or see masterpieces by Gustav Klimt at the Belvedere, this corner of Vienna mixes back-to-nature highs and cultural thrills. Avid shoppers should bring an oversized suitcase and make a beeline for the glut of high-street stores and chichi boutiques lining Landstrasser Hauptstrasse. By night, discover snug brewpubs with creaking beams and hip clubs with urban edge.

SIGHTS & ATTRACTIONS

Augarten

Once an imperial hunting lodge, this Baroque palace overlooks a vast expanse of greenery – a great place for a stroll or picnic when the sun shines. Today the site houses Augarten Porcelain, where you can admire (or buy if you've got the cash) some of Austria's finest handmade ceramics. ⓐ Obere Augartenstr. 1 ⓣ 01 211 24 18 ⓦ www.augarten.at ⓗ 09.30–17.00 Mon–Fri, closed Sat & Sun ⓤ U-Bahn: Taborstrasse U2

Danube boat trip

This round trip along the Danube Canal takes in key landmarks like the Prater and the lofty Danube Tower. The two-hour loop aboard the MS *Vindobona* is a laid-back way to take in the sights.

Reichsbrücke 01 588 80 www.ddsg-blue-danube.at U-Bahn: U1 Vorgartenstrasse

Hundertwasserhaus

The ingenious Viennese architect Friedensreich Hundertwasser went wild with his palette on this 50-apartment housing complex. It's not possible to tour the house, but in the ground-floor café you can watch a film of a tour that shows mirrored tiles, creeping vines and balconies sprouting trees. Löwengasse & Kegelgasse No phone www.hundertwasserhaus.at Film shows constantly 10.00–18.00 daily Tram 1: Hetzgasse

Hundertwasserhaus is a sight to behold

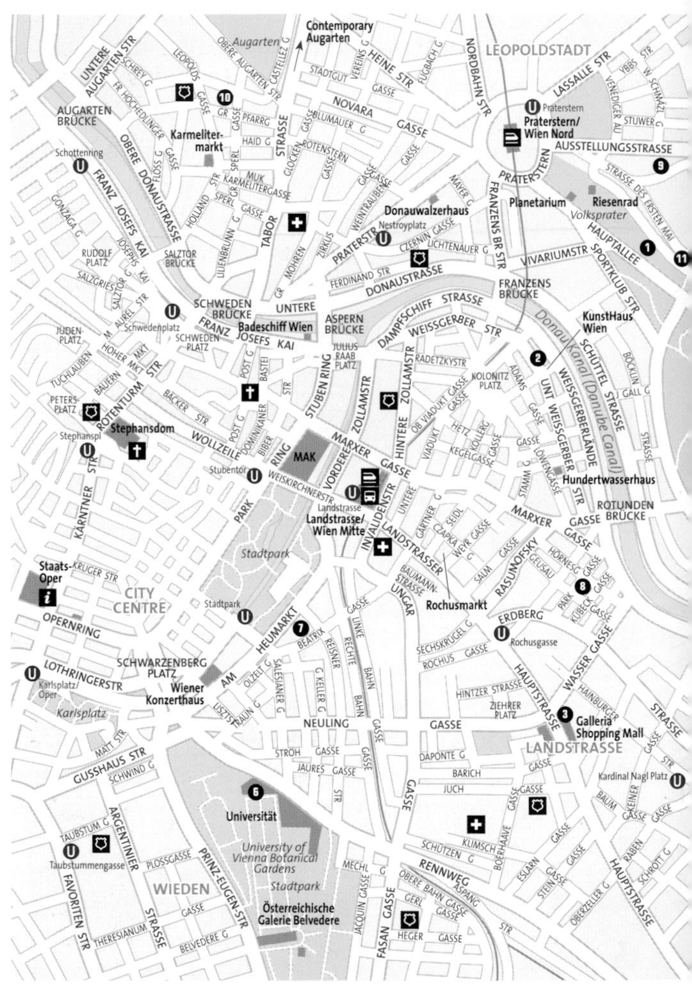
Contemporary Augarten
Augarten
LEOPOLDSTADT
Praterstern/ Wien Nord
Karmelitermarkt
Planetarium
Riesenrad
Volksprater
Donauwalzerhaus
Badeschiff Wien
KunstHaus Wien
Donaukanal (Danube Canal)
Stephansdom
MAK
Hundertwasserhaus
Landstrasse/ Wien Mitte
Stadtpark
Staats-Oper
CITY CENTRE
Rochusmarkt
Wiener Konzerthaus
Karlsplatz
Galleria Shopping Mall
LANDSTRASSE
Universität
University of Vienna Botanical Gardens
WIEDEN
Österreichische Galerie Belvedere
RENNWEG
OPERNRING
SCHWARZENBERG PLATZ
HAUPTALLEE
AUSSTELLUNGSSTRASSE
FRANZ JOSEFS KAI
OBERE DONAUSTRASSE
DONAUSTRASSE
MARXER GASSE
LANDSTRASSER HAUPTSTRASSE
PRINZ-EUGEN-STR
FAVORITEN STR
ARGENTINIER STRASSE

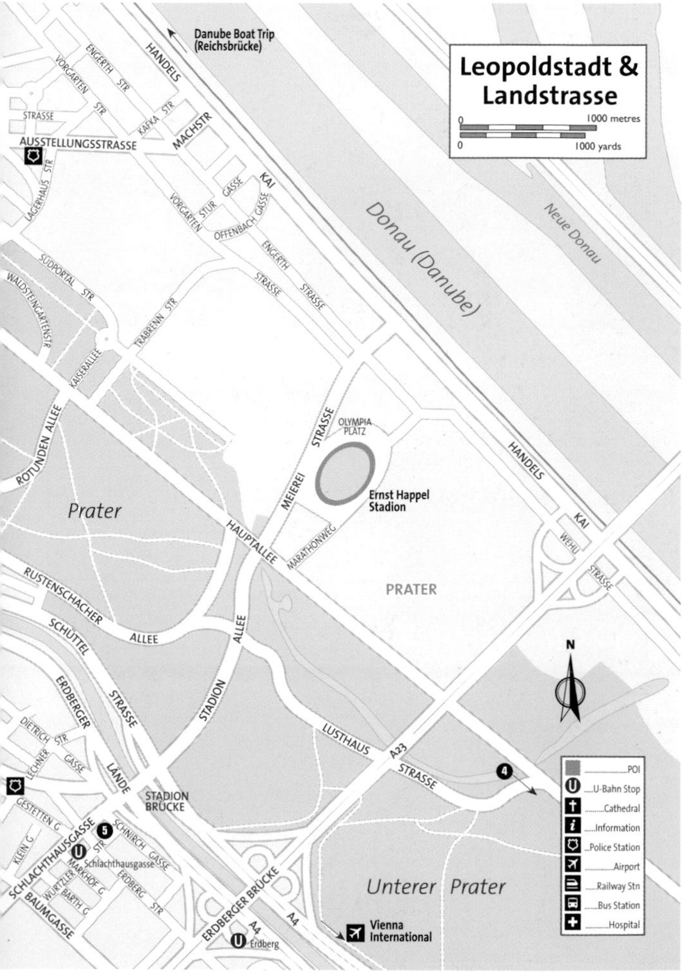

Leopoldstadt & Landstrasse

0 1000 metres

0 1000 yards

Danube Boat Trip (Reichsbrücke)

HANDELS KAI
ENGERTH STR
VORGARTEN STR
STRASSE
AUSSTELLUNGSSTRASSE
KAFKA STR
MACHSTR
LAGERHAUS STR
VORGARTEN
STUR GASSE
OFFENBACH GASSE
ENGERTH STRASSE
STRASSE
SÜDPORTAL STR
WALDSTEINGARTENSTR
TRABRENN STR
KAISERALLEE
ROTUNDEN ALLEE
Donau (Danube)
Neue Donau
MEIEREI STRASSE
OLYMPIA PLATZ
Ernst Happel Stadion
HANDELS KAI
WEHLI STRASSE
Prater
HAUPTALLEE
MARATHONWEG
PRATER
RUSTENSCHACHER ALLEE
SCHÜTTEL STRASSE
STADION ALLEE
ERDBERGER LÄNDE
DIETRICH STR
LECHNER GASSE
LUSTHAUS STRASSE
A23
STADION BRÜCKE
GESTETTEN G
KLEIN G
SCHLACHTHAUSGASSE
Schlachthausgasse
SCHNIRCH GASSE
STR
MARKHOF G
WÜRTZLER
BARTH G
BAUMGASSE
ERDBERG STR
ERDBERGER BRÜCKE
A4
Erdberg
Unterer Prater
Vienna International
N

POI
U-Bahn Stop
Cathedral
Information
Police Station
Airport
Railway Stn
Bus Station
Hospital

RAINBOW REBEL

The rebellious darling of Austrian art and architecture, Friedensreich Hundertwasser (1928–2000) believed that 'colourfulness, variety and diversity are by all means better than the grey, the average grey'. Hundertwasser challenged convention by using clashing colours, crooked windows, reflective mosaics and irregular lines in his painting and his architectural work – putting his controversial stamp on everything from tower blocks and churches to schools and museums.

Prater

Whiffs of candyfloss and the sound of merry-go-rounds fill the air at the Prater, one of the world's oldest amusement parks. Emperor Joseph II opened the park to the public in 1766 and kids (not to mention big kids) still flock to the rides in droves today. ⓣ 01 728 05 16 ⓦ www.prater.at ◷ Amusement park: 10.00–01.00 daily (Mar–Oct) ⓤ U-Bahn: U1 Praterstern

Riesenrad (Ferris wheel)

Vienna shrinks to the size of a postage stamp as you climb high in the Prater's iconic Ferris wheel. Constructed in 1897, the 65-m (213-ft) high wheel rose to fame in the film *The Third Man* and has been one of the city's best-loved landmarks ever since. ⓐ Prater ⓣ 01 729 54 30 ⓦ www.wienerriesenrad.com ◷ 09.00–24.00 daily (summer); 10.00–20.00 daily (winter) ⓤ U-Bahn: U1 Praterstern

University of Vienna Botanical Gardens

An oasis of calm, these botanical gardens nurture a variety of alpine species, plus tropical ferns, swamp plants and orchids. Unusual species to look out for include Russian olives, date plums, tubular red buckeye flowers and Antarctic beech trees.
ⓐ Rennweg 14 ⓣ 01 427 75 41 00 ⓦ www.botanik.univie.ac.at
09.30–dusk daily S-Bahn: Rennweg

Atelier Augarten's sculpture garden

CULTURE

Badeschiff Wien

When the sun's out, join the locals to splash in the 30-m (100-ft) long pool and sunbathe on the deck at the Badeschiff, a ship permanently moored on the Danube Canal. Should you get peckish, there's also a funky restaurant, Holy Moly, serving up fusion cuisine. ⓐ Am Donaukanal ⓦ www.badeschiff.at 🕒 10.00–24.00 daily (June–Sept) Ⓝ U-Bahn: U4 Schwedenplatz ❶ Admission charge

Contemporary Augarten

Contemporary art enthusiasts are in their element at this light-flooded gallery, once the studio of the Austrian sculptor Gustinus Ambrosi (1893–1975) and now the home of the Österreichische Galerie Belvedere (see opposite). A clutch of stone and bronze sculptures by Ambrosi is joined by works from all over the world. Wander through the gardens to spot other abstract Austrian creations. ⓐ Scherzergasse 1A ⓣ 01 795 570 ⓦ www.belvedere.at 🕒 11.00–19.00 Thur–Sun, closed Mon–Wed Ⓝ Tram 2: Am Tabor ❶ Admission charge

Donauwalzerhaus (Johann Strauss House)

Take a look inside the house where Strauss composed the world's most famous waltz in 1867 – *The Blue Danube*. A well-presented collection of instruments, paintings and documents traces his life. ⓐ Praterstr. 54 ⓣ 01 214 01 21 ⓦ www.wienmuseum.at 🕒 10.00–13.00 & 14.00–18.00 Tues–Sun, closed Mon Ⓝ U-Bahn: U1 Nestroyplatz ❶ Admission charge

KunstHaus Wien

Weird, wacky and wonderful, Hundertwasser's art gallery boggles the mind. Patterned with black-and-white tiles, the façade is like a giant chessboard. Inside things get curiouser and curiouser, with uneven floors and irregular lines. ⓐ Untere Weissgerberstr. 13 ⓣ 01 712 04 95 ⓦ www.kunsthauswien.at ⓛ 10.00–19.00 daily ⓝ Tram 1: Radetzkyplatz ⓘ Admission charge

Österreichische Galerie Belvedere (Belvedere Gallery)

This Baroque palace is renowned for its outstanding art collection. The palace is split into two parts: the Upper Belvedere and the Lower Belvedere. The former showcases 19th- and 20th-century works, including Monet and Van Gogh masterpieces and Klimt's *Kiss*. The Lower Belvedere is crammed with medieval, Baroque and Golden Age treasures. ⓐ Prinz-Eugen-Str. 37 ⓣ 01 795 57 134 ⓦ www.belvedere.at ⓛ 10.00–18.00 daily ⓝ Tram D: Schloss Belvedere ⓘ Admission charge

Planetarium

Gaze at twinkling stars and far-flung galaxies in the Prater. Using the latest laser-beam technology, the planetarium's shows evoke an amazingly realistic universe. ⓐ Oswald-Thomas-Platz 1 ⓣ 01 729 54 940 ⓦ www.planetarium-wien.at ⓛ Show times vary so check website for details ⓝ U-Bahn: U1 Praterstern ⓘ Admission charge

Wiener Konzerthaus

This Art Nouveau concert hall is one of Vienna's top addresses for classical music buffs. The venue plays host to names like the Vienna Chamber Orchestra and Vienna Mozart Orchestra. ⓐ Lothringerstr. 20 ⓣ 01 242 002 ⓦ http://konzerthaus.at ⓝ U-Bahn: U4 Stadtpark

RETAIL THERAPY

Burgenland Vinothek This well-stocked vaulted wine store is lined with bottles of fine Austrian Burgenland wines and liqueurs. ⓐ Baumannstr. 3 ⓣ 01 718 25 73 ⓦ www.burgenland-vinothek.at ⓞ 13.00–19.00 Tues–Fri, 10.00–15.00 Sat, closed Sun & Mon ⓝ U-Bahn: U3 Landstrasse-Wien Mitte

Galleria This shopping mall houses everything from Müller, C&A, Lacoste and WMF to a bookstore, nail bar and hair salon. There are also plenty of cafés and restaurants. ⓐ Landstrasser Hauptstr. 99 ⓣ 01 712 94 72 ⓦ www.galleria-landstrasse.at ⓞ 09.00–18.30 Mon–Fri, 09.00–17.00 Sat, closed Sun ⓝ U-Bahn: U3 Rochusgasse

MARKETS

Karmelitermarkt Bustling market where the stalls are piled high with fresh fruit, vegetables and Asian specialities. ⓐ Krummbaumgasse/Leopoldsgasse ⓞ 06.00–19.30 Mon–Fri, 06.00–17.00 Sat, closed Sun ⓝ Tram 21: Karmeliterplatz

Rochusmarkt Fill your bags with fresh fruit, flowers and cheese. ⓐ Landstrasser Hauptstr. ⓞ 06.00–19.30 Mon–Fri, 06.00–17.00 Sat, closed Sun ⓝ U-Bahn: U3 Rochusgasse

TAKING A BREAK

Café Meierei £ ❶ Enjoy breakfast or a light lunch on the leafy terrace of this Prater café. Snacks include Thai stir-fries and smoked salmon with Dijon mustard. ⓐ Hauptallee 3 ⓣ 01 728 02 66 ⓦ www.meierei.at ◷ 10.00–23.00 Mon–Sat, 09.00–22.00 Sun (summer); 11.00–19.00 Mon–Sat, 09.00–19.00 Sun (winter) ⓤ U-Bahn: U1 Praterstern

KunstHaus Wien café restaurant £ ❷ Relax with a drink or snack in the KunstHaus Wien café's lush gardens, a pocket-sized jungle complete with hanging vines, palms and flowers.

Stop for lunch in a mini-jungle: KunstHauswien's café restaurant

ⓐ Weissgerberlände 14 ⓣ 01 595 30 50 ⓦ www.kunsthauswien.com ⓛ 10.00–19.00 daily ⓝ Tram 1: Radetzkyplatz

Tauber Café £ ❸ This café in the Galleria mall whips up great open sandwiches, from egg mayonnaise and smoked salmon to caviar and herring. ⓐ Landstrasser Hauptstr. 99 ⓣ 01 712 04 485 ⓦ www.tauber.at ⓛ 08.00–19.00 Mon–Fri, 08.00–18.00 Sat, closed Sun ⓝ U-Bahn: U3 Rochusgasse

Lusthaus Wien ££ ❹ Surrounded by chestnut trees, this elegant Baroque pavilion is the place to try lemon-and-mint Arabian iced tea with poppy cake or truffle gnocchi with parmesan. ⓐ Freudenau 254 ⓣ 01 728 95 65 ⓦ www.lusthaus-wien.at ⓛ 12.00–23.00 Mon–Fri, 12.00–18.00 Sat & Sun (May–Sept); 12.00–18.00 Thur–Tues, closed Wed (Oct–Apr) ⓝ U-Bahn: U3 Schlachthausgasse

AFTER DARK

RESTAURANTS

Amon's Gastwirtschaft £ ❺ Set around a leafy inner courtyard, this restaurant serves dishes like monkfish on basmati rice and spinach and ricotta *knödel* (dumplings). ⓐ Schlachthausgasse 13 ⓣ 01 798 81 66 ⓦ www.amon.at ⓛ 10.00–24.00 Mon–Sat, 10.00–16.00 Sun ⓝ U-Bahn: U3 Schlachthausgasse

Salm Bräu £ ❻ Sample homebrews and Viennese fare at this brewery restaurant. The meaty menu features Bohemian beer

soup, pork shank and smoked venison ham. Take a pew in the 17th-century Georgsaal or red-brick cellar vault. ⓐ Rennweg 8 ⓣ 01 799 59 92 ⓦ www.salmbraeu.com ◷ 11.00–24.00 daily Ⓝ Tram 71: Unteres Belverdere

StadtParkBräu £ ❼ This bar and restaurant offers traditional food and a great choice of beers and wines. Wander across from the Stadtpark and enjoy a great meal beneath the beautiful, arched ceiling. ⓐ Am Heumarkt 5 ⓣ 01 713 71 02 ⓦ www.stadtparkbraeu.at ◷ 11.00–24.00 daily Ⓝ U-Bahn: U4 Stadtpark

Taverna Lefteris £ ❽ Greek restaurant with a rustic feel. Savour Cretan cuisine including mezze, moussaka or marinated octopus salad with a glass of retsina. ⓐ Hörnesgasse 17 ⓣ 01 713 74 51 ⓦ www.taverna-lefteris.at ◷ 18.00–24.00 Mon–Sat, closed Sun Ⓝ U-Bahn: U3 Rochusgasse

Wieselburger Bierinsel £ ❾ This cheery Prater restaurant has free-flowing beer and a shady terrace where you can tuck into huge steaks barbecued over lava stone or spicy Viennese goulash. ⓐ Prater 11, off Ausstellungsstr. ⓣ 01 729 47 85 ⓦ www.bierinsel.at ◷ 08.30–23.00 daily Ⓝ U-Bahn: U1 Praterstern

Restaurant Vincent ££ ❿ Foodies go gaga over Gerold Kulterer's award-winning cuisine. Decked out in blacks and creams, the décor is minimalist chic and the service snappy. The scallops, trout with almonds and Bresse chicken come recommended. ⓐ Grosse Pfarrgasse 7 ⓣ 01 214 15 16 ⓦ www.restaurant-vincent.at ◷ 18.00–24.00 Mon–Sat, closed Sun Ⓝ U-Bahn: U1 Nestroyplatz

Schweizerhaus ££ ⓫ Wind down a day at the Prater over dinner at this atmospheric beer garden and restaurant. The portions of specialities like *Hintere Schweinsstelze* (roasted pork hocks) and beef goulash are simply enormous. There are also vegetarian and children's options on the menu. ⓐ Prater 116 ⓣ 01 728 0152 13 ⓦ www.schweizerhaus.at 🕒 11.00–23.00 (mid-Mar–Oct) 🚇 U-Bahn: U2 Praterstern

BARS & CLUBS

Aera This urban-chic café near the Danube Canal hosts regular live music from rock to jazz and Latino (see the line-up on the website). It also does good food and weekend brunches. ⓐ Gonzagagasse 11 ⓣ 067 6844 260 270 🕒 10.00–01.00 daily 🚇 U-Bahn: U4 Schottenring

Arena Ear-splitting music rocks the crowd at this popular club which stages rock, metal and punk concerts. There's an open-air cinema in summer. ⓐ Baumgasse 80 ⓣ 01 798 85 95 ⓦ www.arena.co.at 🕒 Opening hours depend on the event being staged so check website for details 🚇 U-Bahn: U3 Erdberg

Club Massiv DJs from the far corners of the globe spin techno and house grooves at this offbeat cellar in the 3rd district. Serious clubbers can dance here till dawn. ⓐ Untere Weissgerberstr. 37 ⓣ 01 714 51 45 ⓦ www.massiv.at 🕒 18.00–late, daily 🚇 Tram N: Hetzgasse

▶ Terraced vineyards are a feature of the Danube Valley

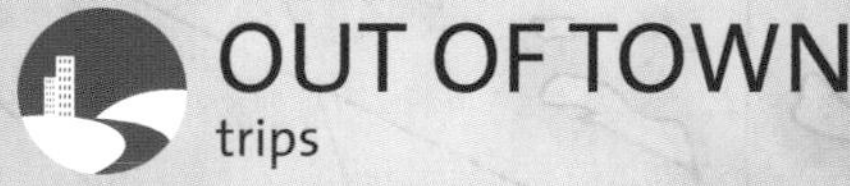

OUT OF TOWN trips

The Wienerwald

Visualise vine-clad hills peppered with caves and limestone cliffs sprinkled with Benedictine abbeys. This UNESCO Biosphere Reserve is a gorgeous pocket of greenery ranging from shady oak forests to Roman spas, vaulted wineries to rare wildlife. Although just a stone's throw from the capital, Vienna's wild and wonderful backyard feels a million miles from the centre's buzz.

If you're looking to add a natural twist and a touch of escapism to your short break in Vienna, the picturesque Wienerwald hits the spot. Hire bikes to cycle through tree-fringed nature reserves or hike the Via Sacra for a cultural overdose. Whether you want all-out action or plenty of pampering, if you go down to Vienna's woods today, you're sure of a big surprise.

GETTING THERE

Bordering west Vienna, the Wienerwald is easy to access. The A1 motorway runs to Pressbaum in 30 minutes, while the A21 connects towns like Hinterbrühl, Heiligenkreuz and Alland. Frequent ÖBB train and bus connections link Westbahnhof station to most towns and villages. The regional public transport network provides timetable details. Ⓦ www.vor.at

SIGHTS & ATTRACTIONS

Allander Tropfsteinhöhle

Tucked into Buchenberg mountain, these 70-m (230-ft) long dripstone caves are a palaeontological site. Don sturdy footwear

Heiligenkreuz

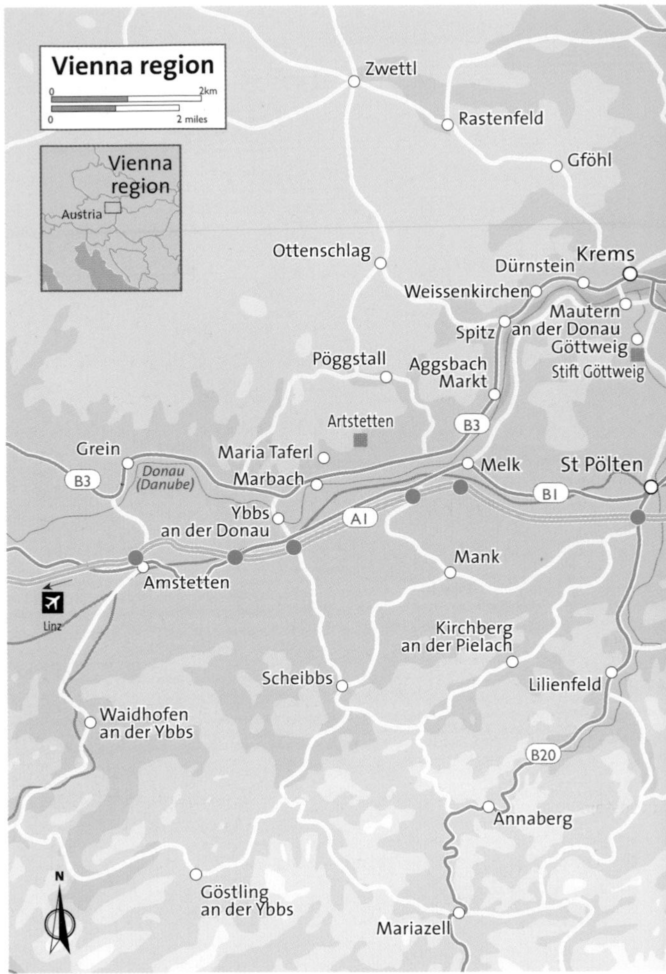
Vienna region
0
2km
0
2 miles
Vienna region
Austria
Zwettl
Rastenfeld
Gföhl
Ottenschlag
Krems
Dürnstein
Weissenkirchen
Mautern an der Donau
Spitz
Göttweig
Stift Göttweig
Pöggstall
Aggsbach Markt
Artstetten
B3
Grein
Maria Taferl
Melk
St Pölten
Donau (Danube)
Marbach
B1
Ybbs an der Donau
A1
Mank
Amstetten
Linz
Kirchberg an der Pielach
Scheibbs
Lilienfeld
Waidhofen an der Ybbs
B20
Annaberg
N
Göstling an der Ybbs
Mariazell

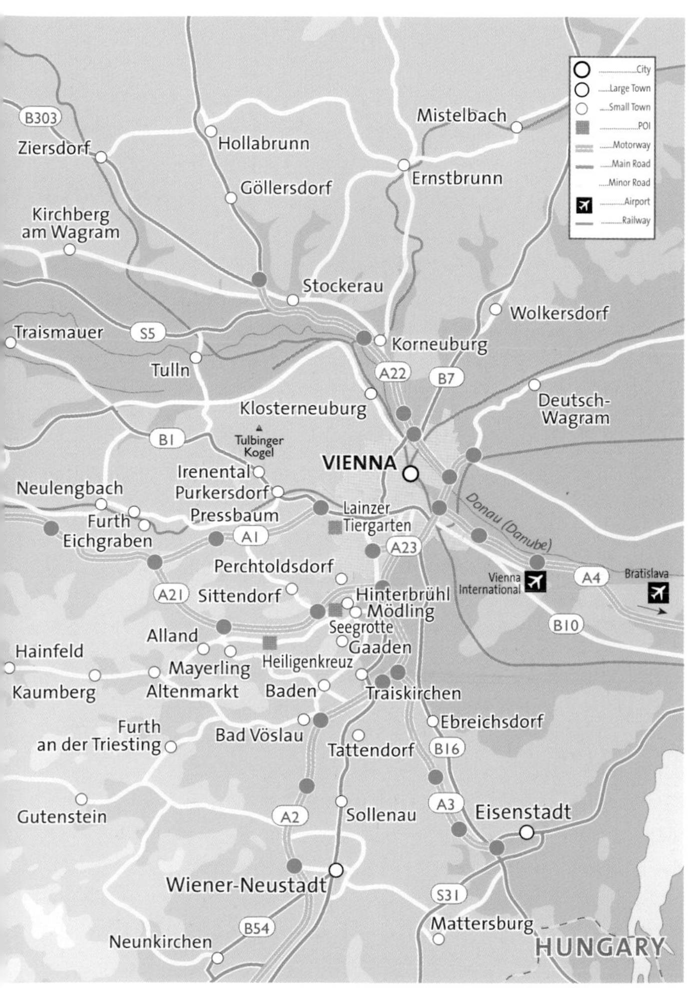

City
Large Town
Small Town
POI
Motorway
Main Road
Minor Road
Airport
Railway
B303
Ziersdorf
Hollabrunn
Mistelbach
Ernstbrunn
Göllersdorf
Kirchberg am Wagram
Stockerau
Wolkersdorf
Traismauer
S5
Korneuburg
Tulln
A22
B7
Klosterneuburg
Deutsch-Wagram
B1
Tulbinger Kogel
VIENNA
Irenental
Neulengbach
Purkersdorf
Lainzer Tiergarten
Pressbaum
Furth
Eichgraben
A1
Donau (Danube)
A23
Perchtoldsdorf
Vienna International
A4
Bratislava
A21
Sittendorf
Hinterbrühl
Mödling
Seegrotte
B10
Alland
Gaaden
Hainfeld
Mayerling
Heiligenkreuz
Kaumberg
Altenmarkt
Baden
Traiskirchen
Ebreichsdorf
Furth an der Triesting
Bad Vöslau
Tattendorf
B16
A3
Eisenstadt
Gutenstein
A2
Sollenau
Wiener-Neustadt
S31
Mattersburg
B54
Neunkirchen
HUNGARY

HOLY HILLS
A magnet for hikers and bikers, the Via Sacra trail weaves from Vienna to Mariazell along a path used by pilgrims over centuries. Crossing meadows, forest and low mountains, and featuring many shrines along the way, the Wienerwald's 29-km (18-mile) stretch passes through Gaaden, Heiligenkreuz, Alland and Kaumberg. The trek is a great way to slip under the region's skin and discover highlights like Gaaden's twin-domed church, the Cistercian abbey of Heiligenkreuz and Alland's dripstone caves. ⓣ 02237 7203 ⓦ www.via-sacra.at

to look at stalactites, stalagmites and the 10,000-year-old remains of a brown bear. ⓐ Buchberg/Alland ⓣ 02258 6666 ⓦ www.alland.at ◷ 13.00–17.00 Mon–Fri, 10.00–17.00 Sat & Sun (July & Aug); 10.00–17.00 Sat & Sun (Apr–Oct) Ⓝ Bus: 365 ⓘ Admission charge

Burg Wildegg

Hike up to this medieval-meets-Renaissance castle surrounded by thick woodlands. The castle's lofty turrets and fortified walls loom large over the valley. ⓐ Sittendorf ⓣ 01 515 52 33 95 ⓦ www.wienerwald.org/p_burg.htm Ⓝ Bus: 364

Dreidärrischenhöhle

Tread carefully in the eerie *Dreidärrischenhöhle*, or 'cave of the three deaf men'. Keep quiet to spot the three species of endangered bats living here. The cave was unearthed in the 19th

century, but closed when World War II broke out. It's now free to visit. ⓐ Gaaden ⓦ www.showcaves.com ◷ Apr–Oct Ⓝ Bus: 365

Föhrenberge Nature Reserve

Marked trails attract walkers and cyclists to this park's limestone crags, open moors and heathland. Look out for umbrella trees, black pines and red squirrels. ⓐ Perchtoldsdorf ⓣ 02236 90253 4426 ⓦ www.naturparke.at Ⓝ S-Bahn: S9; Bus: 260

Heiligenkreuz

Think *The Sound of Music* and this picture-perfect Cistercian abbey won't disappoint. Elegant spires rise above the red-roofed structure, sitting on 900 years of history. Seek out the church's

Burg Wildegg

Romanesque cloister, cross-ribbed vaulting and the Fountain House's Babenberg family portraits. ⓐ Heiligenkreuz 1 ⓣ 02258 8703 ⓦ www.stift-heiligenkreuz.at ⓛ Tours: 10.00, 11.00, 14.00, 15.00, 16.00 Mon–Sat, 11.00, 14.00, 15.00, 16.00 Sun ⓝ Bus: 365 ⓘ Admission charge

Jagdschloss Mayerling (Mayerling Lodge)
This former royal hunting lodge is where Crown Prince Rudolf and his 17-year-old mistress Baroness Marie Vetsera were found dead in 1889. The exhibition reveals more about the famous murder mystery. ⓐ Mayerling, Alland ⓣ 02258 2275 ⓛ 09.00–18.00 daily ⓝ Bus: 365/458

The church and hunting lodge at Mayerling

Klosterneuburg

Perched high above the Danube, the mighty spires and domes of this Benedictine abbey are a sight to behold. Step inside to uncover the giant Baroque organ, centuries-old wine cellars and the astonishing 12th-century altarpiece, painted in 51 panels over a period of 11 years by Nicholas of Verdun – it's one of the world's finest medieval artworks. Ⓐ Stiftsplatz 1, Klosterneuburg Ⓣ 02243 4110 Ⓛ 10.00–17.00 daily Ⓦ www.stift-klosterneuburg.at Ⓝ S-Bahn: S40 Ⓘ Admission charge

Lainzer Tiergarten

This expansive conservation area on the edge of Vienna is perfect for a picnic amid undisturbed nature. Stroll past beech and oak trees to spot wild boar, moufflon and deer. Look out for endangered species including the white-backed woodpecker and fire salamander. Ⓐ Lainzer Tor, 13 Hermesstr Ⓣ 01 4000 49200 Ⓛ 09.00–17.00 (winter), 08.00–dusk (summer) Ⓝ Tram: 60

Leopold-Figl-Warte

This bizarre-looking corkscrew tower on top of the 494-m (1,621-ft) high Tulbinger Kogel mountain twists to a viewing platform that looks out over the treetops. On a clear day you'll get fine views of the Danube, Krems and the alpine peaks of Ötscher, Rax and Schneeberg. Ⓐ Tulbinger Kogel Ⓝ Bus: 449

Römertherme Baden

Take the therapeutic waters at Baden's thermal spa and sauna complex. The glass-roofed pool features whirlpools, massage jets and underwater music. Steam in 95°C (203°F) Finnish saunas and

herbal baths or unwind with a massage in the beauty centre. ⓐ Brusattiplatz 4, Baden ⓣ 02252 450 30 ⓦ www.roemertherme.at ⓛ 10.00–22.00 daily ⓡ Bus: 360 ⓘ Admission charge

Sandstein Nature Reserve

A shady beech forest with a game reserve and nature trails, this expanse of greenery is the place to come eye to eye with free-roaming deer and wild boar. Follow the path to the highest point, 475-m (1,560-ft) Rudolfshöhe, for far-reaching views over the Wienerwald and Vienna. Children love the animal petting area. ⓐ Purkersdorf ⓣ 02231 627 46 ⓦ www.purkersdorf.at ⓡ S-Bahn: S50

Seegrotte Hinterbrühl

This former mine became Europe's largest subterranean lake in 1912 when it was accidentally flooded with 20 m litres (4.4 m gallons) of water. Weave through narrow mining tunnels and see the cobalt blue lake shimmer far below ground. ⓐ Grutschgasse 2A, Hinterbrühl ⓣ 02236 263 64 ⓦ www.seegrotte.at ⓛ 09.00–17.00 (Apr–Oct); 09.00–12.00 & 13.00–15.00 Mon–Fri, 09.00–15.30 Sat & Sun (Nov–Mar) ⓡ Bus: 364/365 ⓘ Admission charge

Steinwandklamm

Steep steps climb this precipitous gorge, with its silvery waterfalls and moss-covered boulders. The 45-minute trek is pleasant even in the summer, since temperatures hover around 10°C (50°F). Don't attempt it with a pushchair! ⓐ Furth an der Triesting ⓣ 02674 882 19 ⓦ www.furth-triesting.at ⓛ Apr–Oct ⓡ Bus: 556

Thermalbad Bad Vöslau

Even the beauty-conscious Romans knew the benefits of Bad Vöslau's thermal springs. Nowadays you can take a dip in 26°C (46°F) waters, test out red-hot Nordic saunas or get active with volleyball and tennis. ⓐ Maital 2, Bad Vöslau ⓣ 02252 762 660 ⓦ www.thermalbad-voeslau.at ◷ 08.00–19.00 (Apr–Oct); 08.00–20.00 (June–Aug) daily Train: Bad Vöslau ❶ Admission charge

Weinstrasse Thermenregion

Hear corks pop on the Wienerwald's wine route. The loop takes in 22 wine-growing villages and spa towns like Perchtoldsdorf, Baden, Sollenau and Tattendorf. Sniff out spicy Zierfandler and zesty Rotgipfler whites in wineries peppering the gently sloping vineyards. ⓣ 02252 707 43 ⓦ www.weinstrassen.at

CULTURE

Stadttheater Baden

This 18th-century theatre stages quality ballet, opera, theatre and musicals. The Sommerarena takes over during the summer. ⓐ Theaterplatz 7, Baden ⓣ 02252 253 2530 ⓦ www.buehnebaden.at ◷ Closed Apr–May; opening hours depend on the piece being staged so check website for details Bus: 360

Wienerwaldmuseum

Culture vultures trace the Wienerwald back to Neolithic times at this intriguing museum housed in a former farm, which contains everything from Iron Age coins to Roman jewellery. Hauptstr. 17, Eichgraben 02773 469 04 www.wienerwaldmuseum.at 08.00–11.00 Wed & Thur, 14.00–17.00 Sat, 10.00–12.00, 14.00–17.00 Sun, closed Mon & Tues Train: Eichgraben-Altlengbach Admission charge

RETAIL THERAPY

Badener Hauervinothek The shelves are lined with 100 local wines at this medieval-style store with vaulted ceilings and tasting tables where you can try before you buy. Pick up a bottle of the burning home-made *schnapps*. Brusattiplatz 2, Baden 02252 456 40 www.hauervinothek.at 10.00–12.30, 15.30–18.30 daily Bus: 360

Made by You Choose a hand-thrown pot, plate or vase at this quirky ceramics workshop, then get painting. There's everything here to create your own mini-masterpiece. Antonsgasse 14, Baden 02252 252 186 www.madebyyou.at 10.00–12.30, 15.00–18.00 Mon–Thur, 10.00–12.30, 15.00–19.00 Fri, 10.00–13.00 Sat, closed Sun Bus: 360

TAKING A BREAK

Backhaus Annamühle £ Cosy café with pastries, coffee and light lunches in the courtyard. Heiligenkreuzergasse 3–5, Baden 02252 485 02 www.backhaus-annamuehle.at 05.30–18.00 Mon–Fri, 05.30–12.00 Sat, closed Sun Bus: 360

Café Central £ This relaxed, wood-panelled Viennese café has served the residents of central Baden for 200 years. Warm up with creamy pumpkin soup or a rum-laced mocha with apple strudel. ⓐ Hauptplatz 19, Baden ⓣ 02252 484 54 ⓛ 07.00–21.00 Tues–Sat, 08.00–21.00 Sun, closed Mon ⓝ Bus: 360

Klostergasthof Heiligenkreuz £ After visiting the abbey, rest beside fountains in the courtyard or take a pew in the beamed restaurant for fresh salads and game specialities with a glass of Grauer Mönch wine. Children's menus are available. ⓐ Heiligenkreuz ⓣ 02258 870 31 38 ⓦ www.klostergasthof-heiligenkreuz.at ⓛ 09.00–22.00 daily ⓝ Bus: 365

Radlertreff Bad Vöslau £ A beloved pit stop of cyclists, this snack bar is the place to refresh with a refreshing Schladminger beer, slurp home-made goulash soup and surf the net. ⓐ Flugfeldstr. 40, Bad Vöslau ⓣ 02252 788 58 ⓦ www.radlertreff.at ⓛ 11.30–20.00 Tues–Sun, closed Mon ⓝ Train: Bad Vöslau

AFTER DARK

RESTAURANTS

Gasthaus Mirli £ Worth a detour, this farmhouse set in orchards tempts with creative cuisine using fresh local, seasonal produce such as asparagus, game and fish. Vegetarians are well catered for. ⓐ Heinratsberg 69, Irenental ⓣ 0664 222 31 31 ⓦ www.mirli.at ⓛ 11.30–22.00 Wed–Sun, closed Mon & Tues ⓝ Bus: 351/408

Panorama Restaurant £ Laid-back restaurant with a lantern-lit terrace, views of the Wienerwald and hearty Austrian fare like beef soup and profiteroles. ⓐ Gumpoldskirchnerstr. 50, Mödling ⓣ 02236 245 41 ⓦ www.panoramarestaurant.at ⓛ 11.00–23.00 daily ⓝ U-Bahn: U6; S-Bahn: S9 Mödling

Höldrichsmühle ££ Dine in the historic vaults of this 18th-century corn mill. Pull up a chair on the terrace beside the stream to enjoy fresh trout or game ragout with Austrian wines. ⓐ Gaadnerstr. 34, Hinterbrühl ⓣ 02236 262 740 ⓦ www.hoeldrichsmuehle.at ⓛ 11.00–22.00 daily ⓝ Bus: 364/365

Trattoria Dazanini ££ A gem of an Italian restaurant where the menu is small but everything is cooked to perfection. Tuck into antipasti, red snapper and raspberry pannacotta. ⓐ Hauptstr. 65, Mödling ⓣ 0664 545 10 46 ⓦ www.dazanini.com ⓛ 12.00–15.00, 19.00–23.00 Tues–Fri, 12.00–15.00 Sat, closed Sun & Mon ⓝ U-Bahn: U6; S-Bahn: S9 Mödling

Villa Nova ££ Wood floors, contemporary artworks and soft lighting create a sophisticated backdrop in this Gault Millau-recommended restaurant. The seasonal menu skips from Austrian to Asian, with dishes such as tuna sashimi on carrot-ginger salad, chanterelle tortellini and moreish marzipan ice cream. ⓐ Helenenstrasse 19, Baden ⓣ 02252 209 745 ⓦ www.stockerwirt.com ⓛ 17.30–23.00 Tues–Sat ⓝ Bus 360

The Wachau Valley

Whether you fancy sipping fruity Rieslings on a gently sloping vine-clad hillside or cruising the snaking River Danube, clambering up to a medieval fortress or marvelling at Benedictine abbeys, the Wachau Valley offers rich pickings. A heady mix of world-class culture and natural highs, this UNESCO World Heritage Site beckons – explore it on foot, by bike, or accompanied by a llama...

Aggstein, perched on cliffs overlooking the Danube Valley

While many people flit past en route to Vienna, it's worth lingering to explore the hidden nooks of this verdant valley that wears every season well. In summer, boats chugging along the river reveal snapshot views of gravity-defying castles, in autumn vines kindle into colour and apple orchards hang heavy, while winter is time to retreat to a cosy *Heurige* (wine cellar).

GETTING THERE

The A22 and S5 motorways link Vienna to the Wachau Valley, an hour's drive away. There are frequent train connections between the Westbahnhof and Franz-Josefs-Bahnhof and towns like Krems (1 hr 10 mins), Melk (1 hr 20 mins) and Ybbs (1 hr 30 mins). ÖBB buses operate an efficient regional service.

SIGHTS & ATTRACTIONS

Aggstein

Clinging to wooded cliffs, this gravity-defying 12th-century fortress affords precipitous views over the Danube Valley. Steep wooden steps lead up to the silver-turreted castle, which was destroyed in 1296 and rebuilt during Renaissance times.
ⓐ Aggsbach ⓣ 02753 822 81 ⓦ www.ruineaggstein.at
◷ 09.00–18.00 (Apr–May & Sept–Oct), 09.00–19.00 (June–Aug), 09.00–17.00 Sat & Sun (Nov) Bus: 1451 ❗ Admission charge

Burg Dürnstein

A rocky path twists up to these medieval ruins, where Richard the Lionheart was held prisoner in the late 12th century until he was freed by his minstrel Blondel. Towering over the pastel-washed town of Dürnstein, the castle has fairy-tale appeal and sweeping river views. Ⓐ Dürnstein Ⓣ 02711 200 Ⓦ www.duernstein.at Train: Dürnstein-Oberloiben

Maria Taferl Basilica

The domed towers of this Baroque basilica, illuminated by night, are a shrine to pilgrims. Inside the church you can admire Antonio Beduzzi's ceiling frescoes and the gilded treasure chamber. The Celtic *opferstein* (sacrifice rock) sits in the square. Ⓐ Maria Taferl Ⓣ 07413 2780 Ⓦ www.basilika.at Guided tours must be pre-booked, see website for details Bus: 7721

Schloss Artstetten

This onion-domed palace towers high above parkland. Once the Habsburgs' summer residence, it is the final resting place of Crown Prince Franz Ferdinand and Sophie, Duchess of Hohenberg. The museum's exhibition traces Franz Ferdinand's life. Ⓐ Schloss Artstetten, Schlossplatz 1 Ⓣ 07413 800 60 Ⓦ www.schloss-artstetten.at 09.00–17.30 daily (Apr–Oct) Bus: 1462 Admission charge

Stift Göttweig

Founded by St Altmann, Bishop of Passau, in 1083, this Benedictine monastery perching high on a hill above the Danube Valley has been dubbed the Austrian Monte Cassino. Ⓐ Furth Ⓣ 02732 855 81 231 Ⓦ www.stiftgoettweig.at 10.00–18.00 daily (Mar–Nov) Bus: 112 Admission charge

Stift Melk

This breathtaking yellow-and-white Benedictine abbey rises like a vision above the Danube. Be inspired by the gold-hued library and Paul Trogers' frescoes in the Marble Hall. In summer, wander past fountains and linden trees in the landscape garden. ⓐ Abt Berthold Dietmayrstr. 1, Melk ⓣ 02752 555 225 ⓦ www.stiftmelk.at
🕒 09.00–17.30 (May–Sept); 09.00–16.30 (Mar, Apr & Oct); open for guided tours in English at 10.55 and 14.55 (May–Oct)
Train: Melk ❗ Admission charge

Tausend-Eimer Berg

Dominating Spitz, this vine-clad hill is nicknamed 1,000-Bucket Mountain because of the amount of wine it can supposedly yield. Tumbling down to the banks of the Danube, the steep terraces

Burg Dürnstein clings to the rocky hillside above Dürnstein

produce some of the region's finest Rieslings. Views from here are pretty intoxicating too. ⓐ Spitz ⓦ www.spitz-wachau.at ⓝ Train: Spitz

CULTURE

Krems Kunstmeile (Cultural Mile)

Art buffs make a beeline for Krems' cultural mile, taking in highlights such as the glass-roofed Kunsthalle, which displays contemporary works alongside Biedermeier masterpieces, the Caricature Museum and a string of other workshops and galleries. ⓐ Krems ⓣ 02732 908 000 ⓦ www.kunstmeile-krems.at ⓝ Train: Krems ⓘ Admission charge

Römermuseum

The town of Mautern goes back to its Roman roots at this intriguing museum with a collection of artefacts unearthed in the 1930s. Look out for the reconstructed kitchen. ⓐ Schlossgasse 12, Mautern ⓣ 02732 811 55 ⓦ www.mautern.at ⓛ 10.00–12.00 Sun–Wed, 10.00–12.00 & 16.00–18.00 Fri & Sat, closed Thur (Apr–Oct) ⓝ Train: Stein-Mautern ⓘ Admission charge

Weinstadtmuseum Krems

Housed in a 13th-century Dominican monastery, this heritage museum houses viticulture-related artefacts, Gothic sculptures and the tiny 32,000-year-old *Fanny vom Galgenberg* statuette, Austria's oldest artwork. ⓐ Körnermarkt 14, Krems ⓣ 02732 801 567 ⓦ www.weinstadtmuseum.at ⓛ 10.00–18.00 Wed–Sat,

RECREATION

Blue Danube Cruise Cruise the Danube to soak up the Wachau Valley's sights from the water. You can buy tickets for the two-hour, 36-km (22-mile) tour from Krems to Melk on board. Shorter trips are also available. ⓐ Handelskai 265, Vienna (info centre) ⓣ 01 588 80 ⓦ www.ddsg-blue-danube.at

Domäne Wachau Savour home-grown wines like Grüner Veltliner and Zweigelt at Dürnstein's age-old cellars. ⓐ Dürnstein ⓣ 02711 371 ⓦ www.domaene-wachau.at ◷ 09.00–18.00 Mon–Sat, 10.00–16.00 Sun (Apr–Oct) Train: Dürnstein-Oberloiben ⓘ Admission charge

Llama Trekking A trekking tour with a South American twist, these one- and two-day llama treks from Göttweig to Melk pass through the Dunkelsteinerwald forest and pause at Maria Langegg monastery. Three- and four-hour treks are also available. ⓐ Diesendorf 28, Melk ⓣ 0650 870 6595 ⓦ www.lamawanderland.at

Rent a Wachau Bike A well-marked cycling path follows the River Danube through the Wachau Valley. This store rents mountain, city and children's bikes at fair rates and can deliver them to your hotel. ⓐ Austr. 50, Mautern ⓣ 0664 214 3512 ⓦ www.rentawachaubike.at

13.00–18.00 Sun, closed Mon & Tues (Mar–Nov) Train: Krems Admission charge

RETAIL THERAPY

Kalt Eis 21 Splurge on designer jewellery. Obere Landstr. 21, Krems 02732 706 47 www.kalteis-21.at 10.00–13.00 Wed, 10.00–13.00 & 15.00–18.00 Thur & Fri, closed Sat–Tues Train: Krems

Wein Handlung Noitz im Kloster Follow your nose to find (and taste) Austria's biggest selection of wines. Undstr. 6, Krems-Stein 02732 70704 www.wein-handlung.at 11.00–19.00 Tues–Fri, 10.00–19.00 Sat, closed Sun & Mon Train: Krems

Wieser Bottles and jars line shelves at this foodie enclave, selling specialities like plum *schnapps*, pumpkin and ginger marmalades, chutneys, coffee, wine and natural cosmetics. Altstadt 39, Dürnstein 02711 805 44 www.wieser-online.at 08.30–18.00 daily Train: Dürnstein-Oberloiben

TAKING A BREAK

Babenbergerhof £ Relax with a light lunch and glass of wine in this manor's cobbled courtyard. The daily menu offers excellent value. Wienerstr. 10, Ybbs 0741 254 334 www.babenbergerhof.at 08.00–21.00 daily Train: Ybbs

Café Hagmann Krems £ A snug café with delicious handmade pralines and pastries. Untere Landstr. 8, Krems 02732 831 67

ⓦ www.hagmann.co.at ⓛ 07.00–18.30 Mon–Fri, 07.00–17.30 Sat, 13.30–18.00 Sun ⓝ Train: Krems

Café Restaurant zum Fürsten £ Dark-wood panelling and low lighting create an old-world feel in this café on the square. ⓐ Rathausplatz 3, Melk ⓣ 02752 52343 ⓦ www.tiscover.at/cafe-madar ⓛ 07.00–22.00 (summer); 08.00–19.00 (winter) ⓝ Train: Melk

Weingut Holzapfel ££ Dine alfresco on the inner courtyard framed by palms and oleander bushes at this award-winning, 700-year-old winery. The home-smoked ham and brook trout in Riesling sauce come recommended. ⓐ Joching 36, Weissenkirchen ⓣ 02715 2310 ⓦ www.holzapfel.at ⓛ 10.00–17.00 Mon–Sat, closed Sun ⓝ Train: Weissenkirchen

AFTER DARK

RESTAURANTS

Florianihof £ Draped in vines, this 14th-century manor serves creative flavours in the vaulted cellar and on the terrace. ⓐ Wösendorf 74, Weissenkirchen ⓣ 02715 2212 ⓦ www.florianihof-wachau.at ⓛ 12.00–14.30, 18.00–21.30 Mon, Tues & Fri, 12.00–21.30 Sat & Sun, closed Wed & Thur ⓝ Train: Weissenkirchen

Gozzoburg £ Overlooking red rooftops, this restaurant dates back to medieval times. The décor is rustic, the vibe relaxed and the food good value – try the flavoursome herring salad. ⓐ Margaretenstr. 14, Krems ⓣ 02732 852 47

ⓦ www.gozzoburg-krems.at ⓛ 11.00–23.00 Wed–Mon, closed Tues ⓣ Train: Krems

Loibnerhof £ Four-hundred-year-old restaurant with lanterns to illuminate the huge tree-fringed terrace. Savour specialities like Wachau fish soup, home-made goose liver pâté and nut *schnapps*. ⓐ Unterloiben 7, Dürnstein ⓣ 02732 828 900 ⓦ www.loibnerhof.at ⓛ 11.30–21.00 Wed–Sun, closed Mon & Tues ⓣ Train: Dürnstein-Oberloiben

Bacher ££ Thomas Dorfer's imaginative take on Austrian cuisine – think Tafelspitz ravioli and succulent rack of lamb with parmesan strudel – has won this place two Michelin stars. Book a table in advance to feast on beautifully presented dishes. There are ten comfortable bedrooms if you decide to make a night of it. ⓐ Südtirolerplatz 2, Mautern ⓣ 02732 829 37 ⓦ www.landhaus-bacher.at ⓛ 11.30–14.00, 18.30–21.30 Wed–Sat, 11.30–21.00 Sun, closed Mon & Tues ⓣ Bus: Mautern

ACCOMMODATION

Gästehaus Heller £ Well located for long hikes through the vines, this cheery hotel offers spotless, light-flooded rooms with satellite TV. Chill out in the peaceful garden and enjoy views over Dürnstein. ⓐ Kremser Str. 14, Weissenkirchen ⓣ 0271 522 21 ⓦ www.tiscover.at/pension.heller ⓣ Train: Weissenkirchen

Marbacher Campingplatz £ Pitch a tent at this leafy campsite which overlooks the Danube and doubles as a watersports centre.

Nearby activities include golf, tennis, cycling and waterskiing. ⓐ Granz 51, Marbach ⓣ 07413 207 33 ⓦ www.marbach-freizeit.at ⓛ Apr–Oct ⓝ Bus: 7721

Barock-Landhof Burkhardt ££ This 16th-century manor screams posh, but rates are surprisingly affordable. Stroll through rose gardens and orchards in the rambling grounds or stop to admire the ivy-clad courtyard. The spacious rooms have minibar, satellite TV and mountain or river views. ⓐ Kremser Str. 19, Spitz ⓣ 02713 2356 ⓦ www.burkhardt.at ⓝ Train: Spitz

Hotel Sänger Blondel ££ This hotel has characterful, large rooms sporting solid wood furnishings and cable TV. When the sun shines, breakfast is served under the chestnut trees in the garden. The restaurant serves up hearty local fare like *Wachauer Rostbraten* (roast beef marinated in wine with apricots and mushrooms). ⓐ Dürnstein 64 ⓣ 02711 253 ⓦ www.saengerblondel.at ⓝ Bus: Dürnstein

Nikolaihof ££ You'll receive a heartfelt welcome at this family-run guesthouse belonging to the Nikolaihof wine estate, Austria's oldest one, dating back to Roman times. The country escape has large, bright rooms with free wireless Internet and flat-screen TVs. Unwind over a glass of organic Grüner Veltliner in the lounge or by the swimming pond framed by vines and apricot trees. ⓐ Nikolaigasse 3, Mautern ⓣ 02732 82 901 ⓦ www.nikolaihof.at ⓝ Bus: Mautern/Donau Rathaus

Schönbrunn Palace used to be Empress Sisi's summer residence

PRACTICAL
information

Directory

GETTING THERE

By air

A number of airlines operate a frequent, direct service between Vienna International Airport (see page 48) and European destinations. A 20-minute journey from the centre, the modern airport offers a full range of services including ATMs, shops and currency exchange. Ryanair flies from London Stansted to Bratislava, 80 km (50 miles) from Vienna (transfer by bus takes around 90 minutes).

Air Berlin ⓦ www.airberlin.com
British Airways ⓦ www.britishairways.com
easyJet ⓦ www.easyjet.com
Germanwings ⓦ www.germanwings.com
Ryanair ⓦ www.ryanair.com

Many people are aware that air travel emits CO_2, which contributes to climate change. You may be interested in lessening the environmental impact of your flight through the charity **Climate Care** (ⓦ wwww.jpmorganclimatecare.com), which offsets your CO_2 by funding environmental projects around the world.

By rail

If you travel by train to Vienna, you'll arrive at Südbahnhof or Westbahnhof. Austria's national rail network **ÖBB** (ⓦ www.oebb.at) runs an efficient service to major cities including Salzburg, Innsbruck and Linz, plus international destinations like Berlin, Paris, Munich, Basel and Bratislava.

By road

Austria's roads and motorways are well maintained. Driving is on the right and international signs are used. If possible, it's wise to avoid rush hour (07.30–09.00 and 16.00–18.00), when roads can get congested. On a clear run you can reach Bratislava in an hour, Graz in two hours and Salzburg in three hours.

National Express and Eurolines operate a service between Vienna and a number of European destinations. Most international and long-distance buses pull into central bus stations like Landstrasse/Wien Mitte, Südbahnhof and Schwedenplatz.

National Express ⓦ www.nationalexpress.com
Eurolines ⓦ www.eurolines.com

ENTRY FORMALITIES

EU, Australian, Canadian, New Zealand and United States citizens must have a valid passport to enter Austria, but do not require a visa for stays of less than 90 days. If you are arriving from another country, you may need a visa and should contact your consulate or embassy before departure. The Austrian Foreign Ministry provides more information on entry requirements. ⓦ www.bmaa.gv.at

It is free to import goods worth up to €175 if travelling by plane, or €300 if travelling by car or train from a non-EU country, but check restrictions on the imports of tobacco, perfume and alcohol. EU residents can import 200 cigarettes, 250 g of tobacco, 10 litres of spirits, 90 litres of wine and 110 litres of beer for personal use. Further information is available at ⓦ www.bmf.gv.at

MONEY

The national currency is the euro (€), broken down into 100 cents. Coins are in denominations of 1, 2, 5, 10, 20 and 50 cents, and of 1 and 2 euros. There are banknotes of 5, 10, 20, 50, 100, 200 and 500 euros.

There are plenty of ATMs in central Vienna where you can withdraw cash with a credit or debit card 24 hours a day. Banks are normally open 08.00–15.00 Monday to Wednesday and Friday, and 08.00–17.30 Thursday. You'll find bureaux de change in banks, airports and the main station. Banks usually offer the best currency exchange rates. Most bureaux de change, travel agencies and hotels accept euro traveller's cheques for cashing.

HEALTH, SAFETY & CRIME

It is generally safe to visit Vienna and there are no particular health risks. No immunisations or health certificates are required, and the tap water is safe to drink.

Austria has a very high standard of medical care. Pharmacies (*Apotheken*) can give medical advice and treat minor ailments and are usually open 08.00–18.00 Monday to Friday and 08.00–12.00 Saturday. Your hotel should be able to arrange for you to see an English-speaking doctor, if necessary.

EU citizens are entitled to free or reduced-cost emergency healthcare in Austria with a valid European Health Insurance Card (EHIC ⓦ www.ehic.org.uk), which entitles you to state medical treatment but does not cover repatriation or long-term illness. There is a charge for routine medical care. All travellers should invest in a good health insurance policy before visiting.

For a city of its size, the crime rate in Vienna is low. However, it's wise to keep an eye on your belongings in crowded areas and on the U-Bahn where pickpockets operate. If you are the victim of a crime, you should inform the police by calling 133 (see *Emergencies*, pages 136–7).

OPENING HOURS

The centre's main shops and malls generally open 09.00–18.30 Monday to Friday and 09.00–17.00 Saturday. Many stay open until 21.00 on Thursday and Friday for late-night shopping. Souvenir shops, bakeries and the shopping centres at Westbahnhof and Südbahnhof stations open on Sunday.

Banks generally open 08.00–15.00 Monday to Wednesday and Friday, and 08.00–17.30 Thursday. Most close at weekends, but many in the city centre have 24-hour ATMs. The bank at Vienna International Airport (08.00–23.00) opens daily.

Most post offices open 08.00–12.00 and 14.00–18.00 Monday to Friday, and some also open 08.00–10.00 Saturday. Vienna's main post office on Fleischmarkt and those located at Südbahnhof and Franz-Josefs-Bahnhof stations stay open longer.

TOILETS

Practically every station, square and street corner has a WC. Keep some spare change handy (usually €0.50) to open the door or tip the attendant. Most conveniences are accessible for travellers with disabilities and have a baby-changing area.

CHILDREN

This child-friendly city is one place little ones will want to stay. Attractions usually offer a 50 per cent reduction for children, and most department stores and public toilets have clean baby-changing facilities, including the public conveniences at Schwedenplatz, Stephansplatz and Volksprater. To locate family-oriented hotels, visit ⓦ www.kinderhotels.com. Budding explorers will love the natural history exhibits at the **Naturhistorische Museum** (ⓐ Burgring 7 ⓣ 01 521 770 ⓦ www.nhm-wien.ac.at). Here they can go back to the year dot to unearth dinosaur skeletons, fossils and minerals – it's a fun-filled museum with an educational twist. Candyfloss, balloons, carousels and an enormous big wheel are the appeal of the Prater (see page 92), where kids love to ride ponies, test out the roller coasters and bounce on the castles. At **Schönbrunn Tiergarten** (ⓐ Maxingstrasse 13 ⓣ 01 877 92 94 ⓦ www.zoovienna.at) kids can smile at crocodiles, venture into the Amazon rainforest and come eye to eye with polar bears and pandas at the world's oldest zoo. At the interactive ZOOM Kindermuseum (see page 81) tots can paint, dance and create music.

COMMUNICATIONS

Internet

There are Internet cafés offering a high-speed, broadband connection all over the centre. Expect to pay anything between €3 and €9 for an hour online. Some cafés and bars with AOL terminals offer free, limited access for customers, including Restaurant Leupold on Schottengasse and Flex café near the Augartenbrücke. Try the following:

Wi-Fi HOTSPOTS

Vienna has wised up to wireless Internet access, with a plethora of cafés, restaurants, bars, hotels and even petrol stations offering the service. Some places offer free access for customers, including **Café Florianihof** (ⓐ Florianigasse 45), **Café Standard** (ⓐ Margaretenstr. 63) and **Levante** (ⓐ Mariahilfer Str. 88A). Other hotspots are:

Am Graben ⓐ Stephansplatz
Bar Italia ⓐ Mariahilfer Str. 19–21
Café Central ⓐ Herrengasse 14
Donauturm Restaurant ⓐ Donauturmstr. 4
MAK Café ⓐ Stubenring 5
Westbahnhof ⓐ Bahnhof Wien West

Big Net Has 18 terminals equipped with MS Office. ⓐ Hoher Markt 8 ⓣ 01 533 29 39 ⓦ www.bignet.at ◷ 09.00–23.00

Café Stein This arty Viennese haunt doubles as a relaxed Internet/ Wi-Fi café where you can surf till the wee hours. ⓐ Währinger Str. 6–8 ⓣ 01 319 72 41 ⓦ www.café-stein.com ◷ 07.00–01.00 Mon–Sat, 09.00–01.00 Sun ⓝ U-Bahn: U2 Schottentor

Speednet Café This ultra-modern venue has some of the speediest connections in town. ⓐ Morzinplatz 4 ⓣ 01 532 57 50 ⓦ www.speednet-cafe.com ◷ 08.00–24.00 Mon–Fri, 10.00–24.00 Sat & Sun ⓝ U-Bahn: U1 Schwedenplatz

TELEPHONING VIENNA
Dial 0043 for Austria, then 1 for Vienna and the five- to nine-digit number.

TELEPHONING ABROAD
To call out of Austria, simply dial 00 followed by the country code and the local number.

Phone

Vienna's public telephones are easy to use and most have instructions in English. You can make international calls from any phone – sometimes with coins but usually with a prepaid phonecard (*Telefonkarte*), which you can purchase from a newsagent, post office or station. A handful of the city's Internet cafés double as call centres and offer competitive rates for phoning abroad. Main post offices feature calling booths where you can speak in privacy. All mobile phones functioning on the GSM standard will be usable in Vienna. For national and international directory enquiries and to speak to the operator call ⓣ 11 88 77

Post

Stamps are sold in post offices and some tobacconists. It costs around €0.65 to send a standard letter or postcard to Europe (20 g) and around €1.40 by economy airmail to North America, Australia, South Africa and New Zealand. Postboxes are bright yellow. Major post offices usually have ATMs and a bureau de change. Vienna's main post office on Fleischmarkt is open

07.00–22.00 Mon–Fri, 09.00–22.00 Sat & Sun. It's possible to locate branches online by entering the postcode. ⓦ www.post.at

ELECTRICITY

Austria has a very reliable electricity system. It is 220 volts, 50 hertz (using round two-pin plugs).

TRAVELLERS WITH DISABILITIES

Vienna's key attractions are wheelchair-friendly and feature accessible toilets, elevators and ramps. These include the Albertina, the Belvedere, the Burgtheater (with dedicated spaces in the auditorium), the Hofburg and the MuseumsQuartier. Most offer concessions (*Ermässigungen*) for visitors with disabilities. The Vienna Tourist Board publishes a handy leaflet in English called Vienna for Visitors with Disabilities, and has plenty of information under Accessible Travel on its website.

Featuring accessible toilets, the best restaurant choices for travellers with disabilities include **Glacis Beisl** (ⓐ Breite Gasse 4), **Café Central** (ⓐ Herrengasse 14) and **Schweizerhaus** (ⓐ Prater).

For further information, consult one of the following:

Australia & New Zealand

Accessibility ⓦ www.accessibility.com.au

Disabled Persons Assembly ⓣ 04 801 9100 ⓦ www.dpa.org.nz

Austria

BIZEPS ⓐ Kaiserstr. 55, Vienna ⓣ 01 523 89 21 ⓦ www.bizeps.or.at

United Kingdom & Ireland

British Council of Disabled People (BCDP) t 01332 295551
w www.bcodp.org.uk

USA & Canada

Access-Able w www.access-able.com
Society for Accessible Travel & Hospitality (SATH) a 347 Fifth Ave, New York t 212 447 7284 w www.sath.org

TOURIST INFORMATION

Vienna Tourist Board

Vienna's English-speaking tourist board is located near the Opera House and provides information, maps and timetables, plus an accommodation and ticket booking service. There are further tourist information desks opposite baggage reclaim at Vienna International Airport and Westbahnhof station.
a Albertinaplatz/Maysedergasse t 01 245 55 w www.wien.info
09.00–19.00 daily

Austria National Tourist Office

This well-illustrated and comprehensive site presents a wealth of information on Austria. Browse for places to stay, themed holidays, sights and attractions, restaurants, events and maps. Brochures can be downloaded online. w www.austria.info

BACKGROUND READING

A Death in Vienna by Daniel Silva. Discover more about Vienna during World War II in this thrilling novel which looks at the none-too-impressive relationship between leading members of the Catholic Church and the Nazis, most damningly with reference to the Holocaust.

The Danube Cycle Way by John Higginson. Get on your bike with this handy guide to cycling the River Danube's well-marked trails – a way of seeing the area that's well worth considering. The book provides many essential details on routes, accommodation and attractions.

The Habsburgs: Embodying Empire by Andrew Wheatcroft. Tracing the rise and fall of the Habsburg empire, this book is a fascinating insight into an incredible dynasty, the antics and machinations of which will keep you engrossed for hours. Proof – if proof were needed – that nice guys rarely finish anywhere but last.

Hundertwasser by Pierre Restany. Dip into this book to find out why wild child Hundertwasser's works and beliefs made such a splash on the Austrian art scene. Not one for those with a frail constitution.

The Lonely Empress: Life of Elizabeth, Empress of Austria by Joan Haslip. This biography takes a peek at Princess Elizabeth's life – a bittersweet, almost fairy-tale, mix of romance and tragedy which captured Austria's heart and which could well inspire the odd tear.

Emergencies

The following are free national emergency numbers:
Emergency services ⓣ 112
Police ⓣ 133
Fire ⓣ 122
Ambulance & medical services ⓣ 144
Emergency doctor ⓣ 141

MEDICAL SERVICES

It's advisable to have a valid health insurance policy before travelling to Austria. EU citizens are entitled to free or reduced-cost emergency healthcare with a European Health Insurance Card (EHIC). Pharmacies (*Apotheken*) are usually open 08.00–18.00 Monday to Friday and 08.00–12.00 Saturday, but at least one in each district stays open 24 hours a day. For details on late-opening pharmacies, call ⓣ 01 15 50 (recorded message in German).

If you need help finding an English-speaking doctor, contact the **Vienna Medical Association Service Department for Foreign Patients** (ⓣ 01 513 95 95). The doctors at **Ambulatorium Augarten** (ⓐ Untere Augartenstr. 1–3 ⓣ 01 330 34 68 ⓦ www.ambulatorium.com) speak fluent English and the surgery accepts credit cards. The centrally located **Vienna General Hospital** (ⓐ Währinger Gürtel 18–20 ⓣ 01 404 000 ⓦ www.akh-wien.ac.at) provides emergency treatment.

POLICE

Each of Austria's nine states has its own police force that deals with public security, traffic control and crime prevention. Like most other EU police forces, officers here wear navy blue uniforms and a white cap with a red-and-yellow trim.

EMBASSIES & CONSULATES

Australia ⓐ Mattiellistr. 2–4 ⓣ 01 506 740 ⓦ www.austria.embassy.gov.au ⓛ 09.00–12.30 & 14.00–16.00 Mon–Fri, closed Sat & Sun

Canada ⓐ Laurenzerberg 2 ⓣ 01 531 38 30 00 ⓛ 08.30–12.30, 13.30–15.30 Mon–Fri

Republic of Ireland ⓐ Rotenturmstr. 16–18 ⓣ 01 715 42 46 ⓛ 09.30–11.30, 13.30–16.00 Mon–Fri

South Africa ⓐ Sandgasse 33 ⓣ 01 320 64 93 ⓦ www.saembvie.at ⓛ 08.30–12.00 Mon–Fri

UK ⓐ Jauresgasse 12 ⓣ 01 716 130 ⓦ www.ukinaustria.fco.gov.uk ⓛ 09.00–13.00, 14.00–17.00 Mon–Fri

USA ⓐ Parkring 12 ⓣ 01 313 39 75 35 ⓦ www.usembassy.at ⓛ 08.00–11.30 Mon–Fri

EMERGENCY PHRASES

Help!	**Fire!**	**Stop!**
Hilfe!	Feuer!	Halt!
Hilfe!	*Foyer!*	*Halt!*

Call an ambulance/a doctor/the police/the fire service, please!
Rufen Sie bitte einen Krankenwagen/einen Arzt/ die Polizei/die Feuerwehr!
Roofen zee bitter inen krankenvaagen/inen artst/ dee politsye/dee foyervair!

ACKNOWLEDGEMENTS

The publishers would like to thank the following individuals and organisations for supplying their copyright photographs for this book: Andy Christiani, pages 19, 21, 31, 42, 47, 83; Dreamstime (Czanner page 8; Danbreckwoldt page 125); Fotozentrum Reiberger, page 13; Erik Holan/KunstHaus Wien, page 97; Brigitte Müller, page 37; World Pictures, pages 17 & 72; Caroline Jones, all others.

The author would like to thank Andy Christiani for his research and Delia Denner at Wien Tourismus for all her help.

Project editor: Jennifer Jahn
Copy editor: Paul Hines
Layout: Trevor Double
Proofreaders: Cath Senker & Jan McCann

Send your thoughts to
books@thomascook.com

- **Found a great bar, club, shop or must-see sight that we don't feature?**
- **Like to tip us off about any information that needs a little updating?**
- **Want to tell us what you love about this handy little guidebook and more importantly how we can make it even handier?**

Then here's your chance to tell all! Send us ideas, discoveries and recommendations today and then look out for your valuable input in the next edition of this title.

Email the above address (stating the title) or write to:
pocket guides Series Editor, Thomas Cook Publishing, PO Box 227, Coningsby Road, Peterborough PE3 8SB, UK.

WHAT'S IN YOUR GUIDEBOOK?

Independent authors Impartial up-to-date information from our travel experts who meticulously source local knowledge.

Experience Thomas Cook's 165 years in the travel industry and guidebook publishing enriches every word with expertise you can trust.

Travel know-how Thomas Cook has thousands of staff working around the globe, all living and breathing travel.

Editors Travel-publishing professionals, pulling everything together to craft a perfect blend of words, pictures, maps and design.

You, the traveller We deliver a practical, no-nonsense approach to information, geared to how you really use it.

Useful phrases

English	German	*Approx pronunciation*
	BASICS	
Yes	Ja	*Yah*
No	Nein	*Nine*
Please	Bitte	*Bitter*
Thank you	Danke schön	*Danker shern*
Hello	Hallo	*Hallo*
Goodbye	Auf Wiedersehen	*Owf veederzeyhen*
Excuse me	Entschuldigen Sie	*Entshuldigen zee*
Sorry	Entschuldigung	*Entshuldigoong*
That's okay	Das stimmt	*Das shtimt*
I don't speak German	Ich spreche kein Deutsch	*Ikh shprekher kine doitsh*
Do you speak English?	Sprechen Sie Englisch?	*Shprekhen zee english?*
Good morning	Guten Morgen	*Gooten morgen*
Good afternoon	Guten Tag	*Gooten tagh*
Good evening	Guten Abend	*Gooten aabent*
Goodnight	Gute Nacht	*Goote naakht*
My name is ...	Mein Name ist ...	*Mine naamer ist ...*
	NUMBERS	
One	Eins	*Ines*
Two	Zwei	*Tsvy*
Three	Drei	*Dry*
Four	Vier	*Feer*
Five	Fünf	*Foonf*
Six	Sechs	*Zex*
Seven	Sieben	*Zeeben*
Eight	Acht	*Akht*
Nine	Neun	*Noyn*
Ten	Zehn	*Tseyn*
Twenty	Zwanzig	*Tvantsikh*
Fifty	Fünfzig	*Foonftsikh*
One hundred	Hundert	*Hoondert*
	SIGNS & NOTICES	
Airport	Flughafen	*Flooghaarfen*
Rail station	Bahnhof	*Baanhof*
Platform	Bahnsteig	*Baanshtykh*
Smoking/non-smoking	Rauchen/ rauchen verboten	*Raukhen/ Raukhen ferboten*
Toilets	Toiletten	*Toletten*
Ladies/Gentlemen	Damen/Herren	*Daamen/Herren*
Bus	Bus	*Booss*